Friend Me! 2

6 get-togethers to deepen Faith & Friendship

Group

Loveland, Colorado

Group resources actually work!

This Group resource incorporates our R.E.A.L. approach to ministry. It reinforces a growing friendship with Jesus, encourages long-term learning, and results in life transformation, because it's

Relational
Learner-to-learner interaction enhances learning and builds Christian friendships.

Experiential
What learners experience through discussion and action sticks with them up to 9 times longer than what they simply hear or read.

Applicable
The aim of Christian education is to equip learners to be both hearers and doers of God's Word.

Learner-based
Learners understand and retain more when the learning process takes into consideration how they learn best.

Friend Me 2!
6 Get-togethers to Deepen Faith and Friendship
Copyright © 2012 Group Publishing, Inc.

Visit our websites: **group.com** and **group.com/women**

This resource is brought to you by the wildly creative women's ministry team at Group. Choose Group resources for your women's ministry, and experience the difference!

Unless otherwise indicated, all Scripture quotations are taken from the *Holy Bible*, New Living Translation, copyright © 1996, 2004. Used by permission of Tyndale House Publishers, Inc., Carol Stream, Illinois 60188. All rights reserved.

ISBN 978-0-7644-7822-2
10 9 8 7 6 5 4 3 2 1   21 20 19 18 17 16 15 14 13 12

Printed in the United States of America.

Contents

Welcome to Friend Me 2!

Are you ready to move from being acquaintances who wave or nod as you pass in the halls or on the street? Ready to move into true friendship with other women and, in the process, move deeper into your relationship with Jesus? If so, *Friend Me 2!* is just for you!

Each week, women will gather for a session that includes food (how can you have a group of women without food included?), Bible, discussion, and prayer. Anyone can be the leader. (We call her the hostess, since that's way more fun and friendly!) Just be sure the hostess reads the session ahead of time and gathers the supplies for that session. Each woman in your group will need her own copy of *Friend Me 2!*

Are We Already Friends?
This resource is a follow-up to the six sessions in the first *Friend Me!* book. You can use *Friend Me 2!* without going through the sessions of the first book, but we do recommend it as a great starting point!

 When you see this icon, the whole group will discuss this together.

 This icon means women will partner or get in smaller groups to share.

Tell Me More!

Friend Me 2! is a flexible six-week series for small groups that compares our friendships with others to our friendship with Jesus. The purpose is to meet new friends in a fun, friendly, nonthreatening way and discover and grow a friendship with Jesus. These get-togethers work for groups of women who are just getting acquainted, for long-time friends, for special-interest groups (such as your scrapbooking group or your prayer team), coworkers, Bible study groups, new attendee groups, and any existing group! You can meet weekly, biweekly, or once a month. You could even supplement your existing weekly small group by experiencing a once-a-month get-together using this book.

How Deep?
Yes, *Friend Me 2!* is great for women who are already Christians. You'll be challenged to go deeper in your faith! But it's also a good starting point for women haven't yet accepted Christ, for those who have expressed curiosity in spirituality, and for those who have put faith on the sideline. The sessions are created to allow conversations at various levels of faith so that anyone can participate and learn.

Where Should I Use This?

Friend Me 2! can be used for home Bible study groups, during the Sunday school hour, or for much larger Bible study groups that meet in your church. In more intimate settings one person can facilitate the get-together. In a larger setting, the hostess can facilitate from the front of the room, with the discussions taking place in smaller groups. Limit each small group to no more than eight people. A group of six to eight guarantees a positive experience and maximum participation by everyone. If you have fewer than six, that's OK too. The experiences will work with smaller groups just as well.

If I'm the Hostess...What Do I Do?

You can have one hostess designated for the entire book, or you may choose to take turns being the hostess. Or you might share the role, having one person prepare the snack while another prepares the experiences. The hostess of the week will need to review the Hostess Prep box at the beginning of each session, as well as the additional tips in the back of each session.

Share the Joy (and the cooking!) If you're meeting in homes, consider rotating from home to home, and have each home hostess prepare the meal or snack for that week.

Each session has an easy snack recommended for your group. But if you'd like to get a little more involved or make it a meal, there are additional suggestions for more elaborate foods that still fit the theme.

More Hostess Tips...

Be yourself. The best leaders are the ones who are comfortable with themselves and willing to be real, vulnerable, and authentic. You're the best you for the job! Then remember that it's not about you. It's about letting God work *through* you. God has put you with specific people in this specific time and place to represent Christ to them.

Be warm and hospitable. If you don't feel comfortable reaching out to others and initiating conversations, join a group but don't lead one.

Be open. Be willing to honestly share your own life stories.

Be willing to share the load. Find a co-leader—a friend who can partner with you.

Now, it's time to *Friend Me!*

Week One

Getting and Giving Love
Experience the love of Jesus and others

Key Verse: 1 John 4:7-8

Hostess Prep

The **bolded sections of text** in each session are for you to read aloud. Feel free to change the wording to make yourself more comfortable. Or just use ours; that's what they're there for.

Provide tissues for this session. For many, this will be a powerfully emotional time as they realize, maybe for the first time, that God has been showing love to them their entire lives.

Invite women to get their food before they sit down.

You'll need:
☐ heart-shaped cookies
☐ watch, clock, or phone with timer
☐ pens

See the hostess helps on pages 14 & 15 for additional tips and other food ideas!

Getting to Know You 🐦
(about 10 minutes)

Enjoy getting to know each other as you're waiting for everyone to arrive. Be friendly and introduce yourself to others you haven't met. While you chat, eat a snack provided by the hostess.

For the next six weeks, we'll be going deeper into ways we can grow closer in friendships with each other and with Jesus Christ. Let's get started with some discussion!

Pass your books around the room, and have each person write her name, phone number, and e-mail address on the "Getting Connected" space (p. 13). You can do this either at the beginning or end of your time together.

🍃 **What could the food we're eating today symbolize about friendship?**

🍃 **What's a loving gesture a friend has shown you this week?**

Today we're talking about the love that friends have for each other, so our food is heart-shaped. Even though it's not Valentine's Day today, we're going to have a bit of a valentine theme. I hope it helps us think more about how we show love to others—and how God shows love to us!

If you're continuing this experience after doing the first *Friend Me!* book, take time now to share about your Getting Real challenges from your last session.

Getting to Know God
(about 45 minutes)

If your group has more than six people, get into smaller groups of four. In your small groups read 1 John 4:7-8 aloud.

> "Dear friends, let us continue to love one another, for love comes from God. Anyone who loves is a child of God and knows God. But anyone who does not love does not know God, for God is love." —1 John 4:7-8

Think of how God has shown you love throughout your life. Be prepared to share with your small group.

Take turns sharing your life story in 3-4 minutes per person. Be sure to include how God has shown his love to you. Your group may want someone with a watch or a phone with a clock to be the designated timekeeper.

Don't rush through the stories, and don't leave anyone out. You'll need to keep an eye on the time, though, so you have plenty of time for the next activity.

When your small group finishes sharing, continue with the next section. You don't have to wait for the other small groups to be ready.

Have the person in your small group wearing the most blue read the verses below. Everyone else, get comfy and close your eyes as you listen.

> "Who shall separate us from the love of Christ? Shall trouble or hardship or persecution or famine or nakedness or danger or sword?…No, in all these things we are more than conquerors through him who loved us. For I am convinced that neither death nor life, neither angels nor demons, neither the present nor the future, nor any powers, neither height nor depth, nor anything else in all creation, will be able to separate us from the love of God that is in Christ Jesus our Lord."—Romans 8:35, 37-39 (NIV)

Spend about 3 minutes silently reflecting on all the stories you've heard today and how each person has experienced God's love in her life. Think about what God would say in a valentine to you. In the space below, fill in God's message to you.

Dear _____

_____

_____

_____

_____

_____

_____

_____

_____

_____

_____

_____

_____

_____

_____

_____

_____

_____

_____

_____

_____

_____

Love,
God

When you're done with your valentine from God, talk in your small group, using these questions as your guide. Feel free to jot down notes as you like.

Q: Why do you think God's love for us is such a big deal?

Q: How is experiencing love from another person like or unlike experiencing love from God?

Chat together until the other small groups are all ready to continue together as one larger group. The hostess will lead everyone at this time.

Getting Real
(about 10 minutes)

We've already taken one step by thinking about and sharing how God has shown us love. Now we're going to look at how we can take what we've learned and act on it this week. Look at the options below, and select the one you'd like to take on this week—or come up with one of your own!

When you've decided on a Getting Real action, share your choice with a partner, and write what you plan to do in the space provided. Make plans right now to connect with your partner sometime in the next week to check in and encourage each other.

+ I'll tell more of my "story" to a friend and ask to hear his or her story.

+ I'll thank someone who has been an important part of my story.

+ I'll read about God's story in the Gospel of John, especially John 3:16-21.

+ I'll set aside 10 minutes to talk to God about my perceptions of him and then ask God to help me discover who he truly is.

Because friendship with Jesus and others is a priority, I'm going to:

_____

_____

_____

Closing

Stand with your group and hold hands while your hostess rereads today's Scripture:

"Dear friends, let us continue to love one another, for love comes from God. Anyone who loves is a child of God and knows God. But anyone who does not love does not know God, for God is love."—1 John 4:7-8

Think of one word that describes your feelings in response to how God has shown love to you; for example, perhaps you feel humbled or excited. Go around the circle and pray, beginning with your hostess. When it's your turn, say your word aloud, then gently squeeze the hand of the woman next to you so she knows you care and that it's her turn to pray.

Your hostess will close by thanking God for everyone in the group and asking God to help everyone become better friends with each other and with him.

Getting Connected

Name: Contact Information:

_____   _____

_____   _____

_____   _____

_____   _____

_____   _____

_____   _____

_____   _____

_____   _____

_____   _____

_____   _____

_____   _____

_____   _____

_____   _____

_____   _____

_____   _____

_____   _____

_____   _____

_____   _____

_____   _____

Week One

Helpful Hints for the Hostess

Especially for the first gathering, set the mood and create a relaxed atmosphere by playing appropriate background music. Consider light jazz, acoustic folk, light classical, or upbeat pop music.

Make sure each woman feels welcome and at home. If you're busy getting last-minute details organized or have a large group, find a warm, friendly woman to be the greeter. Remember, friend-making is a priority for this study! As each new person arrives, introduce her to those who are already there.

For extra impact: Give each woman a paper heart (you can make these from pink or red construction paper) as a reminder to experience and share love in relationships.

Recipe Options

The point of the food choice for this gathering is that women will find a variety of ingredients in their snack or meal. Each ingredient offers something unique to the taste. In the same way, each person brings something unique to a group of friends.

Easiest Option:
♥ heart-shaped cookies
♥ beverages

Purchase heart-shaped cookies from a local bakery or grocery store.

Easy+ Option:

- heart-shaped muffins
- beverages

Use a recipe for berry muffins that you like. If you have heart-shaped muffin tins, use those. But if not, here's a trick you can use. Use foil cupcake liners in your muffin tins. Spoon the muffin batter into the liner, so it's about two-thirds full. Place a marble between the foil liner and the muffin tin. Bake as your recipe directs.

Note: If you don't have marbles, simply frost the muffins and use red candies to form a heart on top of each muffin.

If you like, frost the muffins with this topping:
Beat together 3 ounces softened cream cheese, 1 tablespoon warm water, 1 teaspoon vanilla extract, and 3 cups sifted powdered sugar. Tint frosting with red food coloring so it turns pink.

Make It a Meal:

- heart-shaped pizza
- heart cake
- beverages

Use any recipe you like for pizza dough, or purchase pre-made dough from the store. Shape it into a heart on your baking pan, and add any pizza toppings your group enjoys. Share the responsibility for this by having each woman bring a topping to add to the pizza. Bake according to the dough recipe directions, and serve while hot!

An easier option would be to top a frozen grocery store pizza with heart-shaped pepperoni. Use scissors to cut each slice of pepperoni into a heart shape. Or ask a pizza restaurant if they will make a heart-shaped pizza.

For a heart cake, bake a pink cake using a store-bought mix or recipe that you like. Cool completely. Frost with purchased pink frosting. Use red candies and red decorator sugar to form a large heart shape on top of the cake.

Week Two

Getting Acceptance
Discover unconditional acceptance with Jesus and others.

Key Verse: 1 Samuel 16:7

Hostess Prep

Review the sticky-note activity in this session, and adapt it to fit your group and time frame. You may want to do it in smaller groups of three or four. Or you may want the entire group to sit in a circle and have each woman write only one sticky note (perhaps for the person on her left), which will save time and still be meaningful.

You'll need:
- ☐ bagels and toppings
- ☐ pens
- ☐ sticky notes

See the hostess helps on pages 24-26 for additional tips and other food ideas.

Getting to Know You

(about 15 minutes)

Enjoy getting to know all of your group members as you're waiting for everyone to arrive. While you chat, eat a snack provided by the hostess. Then begin your get-together with these discussion questions:

🍂 **What is strange about today's food?**

🍂 **Tell about a time you felt like you didn't belong.**

Part of what we're eating doesn't seem to quite belong. It may not be like the other parts or live up to our usual expectations. That's something many of us have felt in real life. Today we're going to discuss what it means to be an accepting friend, and we'll explore why Jesus is the most accepting and loving friend we could have.

Before we dive in, let's check in on the Getting Real challenges from last week.

Share with the entire group how you followed through with your commitment and what happened as a result.

Getting to Know God

(about 25 minutes)

Play a "handshake" game with your group. When your hostess calls "Meet!" find someone who fits the first bullet point below. Shake that woman's hand. Each time your hostess calls "Meet!" find a new partner who fits the next bullet point.

* Someone who's wearing the same color you're wearing

* Someone who has a birthday in the same month as yours

* Someone who shares your favorite television show

* Someone who's wearing the same kind of shoes as you

* Someone who plays a sport that you also play

* Someone who shares a favorite pizza topping

* Someone who's read a book you've just finished

Form groups of four, and discuss the questions below. If you'd like, make notes in the space provided.

Q: How can we relate this activity to the process of acceptance?

Q: Consider this statement: It's hard to completely accept people who are different from us. Do you agree or disagree? Why?

The person wearing the most red in your small group should read the following paragraph aloud:

> For some of us, discovering "sameness" is the key to acceptance—because it's easier and more comfortable to accept people with whom we have something in common. We might feel like we deserve friends who are like us, and vice versa. For others of us, similarities don't have a huge part in how we accept people and build friendships; we have other expectations.

Take a moment to silently jot down answers to these questions:

Q: I feel accepted when someone…

Q: I feel like I'm not accepted when someone…

With your group of four, talk about what you wrote, and discuss the questions below:

Q: Based on your answers, how would you define unconditional acceptance?

Q: How has God shown you unconditional acceptance?

Get back together with your whole group. Your hostess will read aloud 1 Samuel 16:7.

"The Lord doesn't see things the way you see them. People judge by outward appearance, but the Lord looks at the heart."—1 Samuel 16:7

Discuss this question:

🍂 **From this verse, what do you discover about God's acceptance for you?**

Using your nondominant hand, write something good God might see when he looks at your heart. This could be a character quality, such as "compassionate" or "truthful." Or it could be something else God might value about you, such as "eager to grow" or "searching for answers."

What's in My Heart

After everyone has done this, discuss these questions together:

🍂 **Why is it important that the messiness and awkwardness of what you've written does not take away from its meaning?**

🍂 **From this experience, what might we discover about God's acceptance?**

Just as awkward writing doesn't take away from the truth and value of what we wrote, our flaws don't take away from the truth and value of who we are. God knows we're not perfect, yet he unconditionally loves and accepts each one of us.

Sit in a circle with your group, leaving room in the center. One by one, each woman will get a chance to sit in the center of the circle and be "stickied." The rest of the group will jot a word or phrase of encouragement for whoever is in the center—something you appreciate about that person. Then you'll stick your encouraging note on her and say aloud what you wrote.

Keep taking turns until each woman has had a chance to be affirmed in the center of the circle.

🍂 **What did this experience show about how others can help you receive Jesus' unconditional acceptance?**

Getting Real 🍂 ─────────────
(about 10 minutes)

We've already taken one step by accepting ourselves and each other. Now we're going to look at how we can take what we've learned and act on it this week. Look at the options below, and select the one you'd like to take on this week—or come up with one of your own!

When you've decided on a Getting Real action, share your choice with a partner and write what you plan to do in the space provided. Make plans right now to connect with your partner sometime in the next week to check in and encourage each other.

🍂 I'll write a note to someone, affirming that person's value and describing why I appreciate him or her.

🍂 I'll reach out to someone I've been having a hard time accepting.

🍂 I'll make a list of my flaws and then give them over to God in prayer. Afterward, I'll cross them out and give thanks for God's unconditional acceptance!

🍂 I'll find a quiet place to write in a journal about Psalm 139:1-18.

Because friendship with Jesus and others is a priority, I'm going to:

_____

_____

_____

_____

Closing

Do this activity silently and prayerfully.

Point to something in the room that's about 20 feet away. Imagine that what you're pointing to is a friendship target you've been aiming at. It may be what you think you need in order to be accepted or to accept others. This item will represent what's preventing you from unconditional acceptance.

Close one eye and see how the object moves away from your finger. Open that eye, and close the other eye. Watch your target move again. Next, put your arm down, and reflect for a moment on God's love and acceptance.

We may think we know the target we need to hit so that we can be fully loved and fully accepted. But Jesus is our target; Jesus never moves and offers us perfect love just as we are.

Close your eyes and pray as a group, thanking Jesus for his unconditional acceptance and love and asking God to help each woman receive that acceptance and love.

Week Two

✿ Helpful Hints for the Hostess ✿

In our conversations about the meaning of the food, some people didn't guess the topic and were initially disappointed about being "wrong." But there are no wrong or right answers in these brainstorming discussions. Make this investigative guessing open and fun; affirm all ideas so no one feels discouraged!

When we did the handshake activity, the participants exchanged hugs instead of shaking hands. Choose a form of greeting that will work best for your group dynamics. What about high fives?

When discussing unconditional acceptance, explore the difference between accepting a *person* and accepting everything that person does. Help women understand how they can choose to accept someone because the person is valuable but not condone everything the person does. Emphasize that this is the nature of Jesus' love and acceptance for us!

The sticky-note activity was a very powerful experience in our group; people were absorbed, laughing, and sincerely encouraging each other. View this as a good example of how others' love and acceptance lead us to Jesus!

✿ Recipe Options ✿

In each of today's food options, there is something unusual that doesn't seem to belong. This will help everyone talk about feeling that they don't belong and the unconditional acceptance that Jesus offers us and that we can offer to others.

Easiest Option:
❀ bagels and toppings
❀ beverages

Purchase a variety of bagels and toppings.

Toppings might include expected ones such as flavored cream cheeses, jams, and jellies. But also include some unusual toppings such as hummus, goat cheese, peanut butter, Nutella (a cocoa and hazelnut spread), and cake frosting. Set out sharp knives and cutting boards. You may want to provide a toaster, too.

Easy+ Option:
* chocolate zucchini cake
* beverages

Zucchini is not something we usually mix with chocolate! But it's actually very tasty.

Make chocolate zucchini cake using the following:

2½ cups flour

½ cup cocoa

2½ teaspoons baking powder

1½ teaspoons baking soda

1 teaspoon cinnamon

½ teaspoon salt

¾ cup butter or margarine

2 cups sugar

3 eggs

1 teaspoon vanilla

½ cup milk

2 cups shredded zucchini

1 cup chopped walnuts

1 cup chocolate chips

Preheat oven to 350° F. Combine all dry ingredients except the sugar. In another bowl, cream the sugar and butter until fluffy. Beat in one egg at a time. Stir in vanilla. Add dry ingredients, alternating with milk. Stir in the zucchini and nuts. Pour into a greased and floured 9x13 cake pan. Sprinkle chocolate chips on top. Bake 50 to 60 minutes until cake tests done. (Stick a toothpick in the center; if it comes out clean, the cake is done. If the toothpick comes out gooey, cook for 5 more minutes, or until the toothpick comes out clean.)

Make It a Meal:

* "gourmet" fast food
* beverages

Set the table with your nicest linens, china, crystal, and silverware. If you don't own nice china, find some you can borrow. Provide fresh flowers for a centerpiece.

Pour soda into nice pitchers and keep in the refrigerator. Purchase plain hamburgers, cheeseburgers, and french fries from your favorite fast-food restaurant. Put the food on platters, and keep the platters warm in the oven until the group is seated and the blessing has been asked. Then bring out the pitchers of soda and the platters of fast food and serve each person.

It's very important that no one sees the food beforehand. The women should only see an elegantly set table. Don't give anyone any clues about what the food is or isn't—the surprise of serving plain fast-food hamburgers on china will make a huge impact on the group!

Week Two

Week Three

Getting Comfort

Find healing in the love of Jesus and others.

Key Verse: Romans 5:6-11

Hostess Prep

Before the gathering, cut one person shape from paper for every group of six people.

You'll need:

- ☐ peanut brittle
- ☐ pens
- ☐ person shapes cut from paper (1 shape per 6 people)
- ☐ transparent-tape dispensers (1 per 6 people)
- ☐ wrapped Band-Aids (1 per person)

See the hostess helps on pages 36-39 for additional tips and other food ideas.

Getting to Know You ✿
(about 15 minutes)

Enjoy getting to know all of your group members as you're waiting for everyone to arrive. While you chat, eat a snack provided by the hostess. Then begin your get-together with these discussion questions:

🌿 **What are some characteristics of our food today?**

🌿 **What are some ways you feel like today's food?**

Our snack was fragile and easily broken. Today we're going to talk about brokenness. We'll discuss some of our hurts and failures and explore what it means to be broken yet loved completely. Before we dive in, let's check in on the Getting Real challenges from last week.

Share with the entire group how you followed through with your commitment and what happened as a result.

Getting to Know God ✿
(about 25 minutes)

Find a partner, and exchange stories about a visible scar you have.

After that discussion, take a few minutes of silent and personal reflection. Think of the pieces of your life that represent deeper imperfections and brokenness. Write a different hurt on each piece of the broken clay pot in the picture.

Come together with the whole group, and discuss these questions:

🍃 **What are different ways we experience hurt?**

🍃 **How do you think we might experience God's presence in these hurts?**

Form a group of six, and get a paper person for the group from your hostess.

We're going to say mean things to our paper people. Maybe they're things people have said to you, or they might be things you've said to others; for example, "You're so stupid!" Each time you say something mean to your paper person, rip a piece of that person off.

In your group of six, take turns saying—in a word or phrase—a hurtful thing that people say or do to one another. As you say your mean phrase, tear a piece from the paper person, and then hand the torn paper person to someone else. Continue until your paper person has been torn by each person in your group.

Read Ephesians 4:29 aloud in your small group:

> "Don't use foul or abusive language. Let everything you say be good and helpful, so that your words will be an encouragement to those who hear them."
> —Ephesians 4:29

Now get a tape dispenser for your group from your hostess. Take turns passing the paper person around again, this time mentioning a kind thing that people can say or do to one another. As you share, use the tape to repair one rip in the paper person. When your paper person has been taped back together, discuss the following questions in your small group.

Q: Compare how your paper person looked before the activity to how she looks now.

Q: How do you resonate with what the paper person went through?

Q: How has God "taped you up" where others have "ripped" you?

After your discussion, your hostess will gather the larger group together again.

We've talked about our visible scars and about the power we hold to tear down or build each other up. Now let's talk about invisible scars. Get back together with the person you talked about scars with earlier.

With your partner, share one invisible scar with each other—something that has hurt you deep inside but that you are willing to share with another woman. Then discuss with your partner:

Q: During this experience, what did you discover about your invisible hurts and scars?

Q: How might we understand our friends' brokenness and love them the way Jesus loves them?

Read Romans 5:6-11 aloud with your partner:

> "When we were utterly helpless, Christ came at just the right time and died for us sinners. Now, most people would not be willing to die for an upright person, though someone might perhaps be willing to die for a person who is especially good. But God showed his great love for us by sending Christ to die for us while we were still sinners. And since we have been made right in God's sight by the blood of Christ, he will certainly save us from God's condemnation. For since our friendship with God was restored by the death of his Son while we were still his enemies, we will certainly be saved through the life of his Son. So now we can rejoice in our wonderful new relationship with God because our Lord Jesus Christ has made us friends of God."— Romans 5:6-11

Discuss this question with your partner:

Q: What does this passage teach you about how Jesus can help you with your invisible scars?

Getting Real
(about 10 minutes)

Your hostess will ask everyone to gather as a whole group.

We've already taken one step by recognizing our brokenness and seeing how Jesus can heal us. Now we're going to look at how we can take what we've learned and act on it this week. Look at the options below, and select the one you'd like to take on this week—or come up with one of your own!

When you've decided on a Getting Real action, share your choice with a partner and write what you plan to do in the space provided. Make plans right now to connect with your partner sometime in the next week to check in and encourage each other.

- I'll avoid criticizing or correcting someone unnecessarily. Instead, I'll offer kind words and build up the person with encouragement.

- I'll describe an emotional scar or tell a story of my own brokenness to someone this week. I'll talk about how God has healed (or is healing) me.

- I'll pray daily for my invisible-scar partner, particularly for comfort from Jesus.

- I'll find my favorite, most comfortable place to relax and focus on Jesus' love as I read Romans 8:35-39.

Because friendship with Jesus and others is a priority, I'm going to:

Closing

Go through this prayer experience in a quiet and reflective mood.

Get a wrapped Band-Aid and a pen from your hostess. Get back together with the partner you shared scar stories with. Write your own name on the Band-Aid, and exchange Band-Aids with your partner. Then take a minute or two to pray silently that Jesus will heal your partner's invisible hurts and scars.

Your hostess will close with this prayer:

Jesus, we know that we've been hurt and that we've hurt others. You are the God of restoration, repair, and healing. Thank you for dying on the cross so that your grace can wash away our sins. We accept your healing and ask you to forgive us where we've hurt others. Amen.

Take your Band-Aid home as a reminder for you to pray for your partner and to follow through on your Getting Real challenge. Keep it in your purse, bag, or wallet as a reminder. And it's always good to have a Band-Aid—just in case!

Week Three

⟡ Helpful Hints for the Hostess ⟡

We tested the paper person activity with a wide range of people—new Christians, people hurt by church, people involved in church all their lives, people questioning their relationship with Jesus—and they all opened up more than ever while being very affected by the activity. View it as an "equalizing" experience, fitting all backgrounds and spiritual levels in your group. It might be very difficult for some people to say something deliberately hurtful. Use this emotional reaction to connect the activity to real life.

You can explore Romans 8:28 in addition to Ephesians 4:29 while discussing the paper-person activity. This verse provides insight into how God can work everything (even the most painful things) together for the best. What a great opportunity to talk about how God loves us and "tapes" us together!

Sometimes it's impossible to put the paper person back together, so don't make this your goal. The purpose of the activity is for people to find meaning in the taping process—whether it is completed or not. However, people may be really intent on taping the person back together perfectly because they don't want it to be a sloppy "fix"—which would provide a good opportunity for further discussion. Ask, "How is this like the way God views and treats us?"

If people struggle with identifying invisible scars, tell them to think of anything that caused them to feel hurt, ashamed, or a sense of failure. The invisible scar could be something specific, such as a relationship problem or a work, school, or church situation. Or it could be a general area of struggle, such as trust, acceptance, or making friends. Emphasize that the purpose of this activity is not to feel discouraged or wallow in hurts. Instead, sharing pain and brokenness with a friend helps open the door to Jesus' healing and unconditional love.

As you discuss the hurts, shame, and failures of life, be aware that some people may not have realized—or be willing to admit—that they are broken. Spend a few minutes exploring 1 John 1:8-9 aloud, and discuss what truths this passage teaches about our brokenness. Allow people to discover or face the brokenness, hurts, and failures they may have been avoiding their entire lives.

Recipe Options

Today's get-together is about finding comfort in Jesus despite our brokenness and imperfections. Jesus can take our troubled, broken lives and create something beautiful! All of today's food includes some kind of "breaking."

Easiest Option:
+ peanut brittle
+ beverages

Purchase peanut brittle to serve. Invite each woman to break off several pieces of the peanut brittle to eat.

Easy+ Option:
+ Broken Glass Dessert
+ beverages

Make 16 servings of Broken Glass Dessert using the following:
5 small packages of different colors of gelatin
1 large package of lemon gelatin
1 large tub of non-dairy whipped topping
6 graham crackers
½ cup sugar
6 tablespoons butter or margarine

At least 24 hours before serving, prepare each of the five packages of gelatin separately, using 1½ cups boiling water per package. Refrigerate several hours until set. When set, cut the gelatin into cubes, and put the cubes in a 9x12 glass pan. Mix the large package of lemon gelatin with 2 cups of boiling water. Cool to room temperature. Gently fold the lemon gelatin into the whipped topping. Pour onto the cubed gelatin. Use a spatula to push the whipped topping mixture between the gelatin cubes and spread it on top. Crush the graham crackers in a food processor, and mix with sugar. Toss the crumbs with melted butter or margarine, and sprinkle the graham cracker crumbs on top of the whipped topping. Refrigerate for at least 6 or 7 hours to set. Cut into squares to serve.

Make It a Meal:
+ Crunchy Chicken Salad
+ rolls and butter
+ beverages
+ cookies

Make 8-10 servings of Crunchy Chicken Salad using the following:

one 16-ounce package three-color deli coleslaw (mixture of green cabbage, carrots, and red cabbage)

two 16-ounce packages broccoli coleslaw (mixture of shredded broccoli, carrots, and red cabbage)

2 bunches of green onions (slice whites and greens)

3 cups slivered or sliced almonds

1 can of real bacon bits

3 cups cherry tomatoes, halved or quartered if they're large

6 boneless, skinless chicken breasts, grilled or sautéed in a small amount of vegetable oil

4 packages chicken or chicken teriyaki ramen noodles

½ cup vegetable oil

3 tablespoons vinegar

3 tablespoons sugar

Salad can be assembled up to 1 hour before serving. Combine the vegetable oil, vinegar, sugar, and the flavor packets from the ramen noodles and mix well to make the dressing. Divide the coleslaw mixes and the green onions between two large serving bowls. Divide the dressing between the two serving bowls. Toss well. On top of the salads, layer the cherry tomatoes, bacon bits, and almonds, dividing the amounts between the two bowls. Chop the cooked and cooled chicken breasts into very small pieces. Layer the chicken on top of the almonds. Put the salads in the refrigerator until time to serve.

When it's time to serve, place the salads on the table. Put the dry ramen noodle blocks on a plate next to the salads.

It's very important not to add the ramen noodles to this salad beforehand. The women will break the noodles into the bowl and toss the salad to help them discover important truths about our "brokenness" before God.

Week Four

Getting Comfortable With Yourself
Learn to be open to Jesus and others.

Key Verse: Psalm 139:1-6

Hostess Prep

Cue the *Shrek* DVD to scene 6 and preview it. You'll need to be ready to stop it when Shrek says "Bye-bye. See you later." (There's mild profanity just after that.)

You'll need:

- ☐ filled doughnuts
- ☐ pens
- ☐ Shrek DVD, DVD player, TV
- ☐ 2 sealed packets of Alka-Seltzer
- ☐ large glass of water

See the hostess helps on pages 48 & 49 for additional tips and other food ideas.

Getting to Know You

(about 15 minutes)

Enjoy getting to know all of your group members as you're waiting for everyone to arrive. While you chat, eat a snack provided by the hostess. Then begin your get-together with these discussion questions:

🍁 **How is the food we're eating today like friendship?**

🍁 **Describe whether you're a closed book or you wear your heart on your sleeve. Give real-life examples.**

Today's food has several different kinds of fillings. You didn't know what you'd get until you started eating. People often don't reveal all of themselves to others. It's not until we trust each other as good friends that we discover some of these hidden things about each other. Today we'll talk about the role trust plays in being open with each other. Before we dive in, let's check in on the Getting Real challenges from last week.

Share with the entire group how you followed through with your commitment and what happened as a result.

Getting to Know God

(about 25 minutes)

Find a partner, and share at least three things that your partner doesn't know about you. (Choose things you'll feel comfortable sharing with the whole group later.) For example, maybe your partner doesn't know that you hiked three-fourths of the Appalachian Trail or once parachuted out of an airplane.

Then discuss these questions with the whole group:

🍂 **What did you learn about your partner?**

🍂 **What was easy or hard about sharing in this experience?**

We're going to watch a movie clip about openly expressing who we are. *Shrek* is a movie about an ogre who lives in a swamp. Shrek is a loner—he's a little different from most folks and has had some trouble being accepted. He has decided that it's much easier to live alone than to risk the disapproval he has encountered in the past. At the beginning of the movie, he encounters a talking donkey who insists on being his friend and companion on a noble quest. Let's see what Shrek has to say.

Watch scene 6 of *Shrek*, provided by your hostess.

Discuss these questions:

🍂 **What did Shrek mean when he said he had "layers"?**

🍂 **Why are ogres and people reluctant to share their layers with others?**

My Layers

Write some of your own "layers" next to the onion illustration below.

Turn to a partner, and talk about your layers.

When you're done, join with another pair to form a group of four, and discuss these questions:

Q: What was it like to share the layers of who you are with someone else?

Q: What risks and rewards come with sharing who we really are?

Turn back to your partner, and affirm her by mentioning one thing you really like about the layers she revealed in the onion activity.

Your hostess will gather everyone as a large group again.

Let's explore this idea of being transparent with others. This demonstration will give us lots of insights into revealing our inner selves to others.

Your hostess will unwrap one Alka-Seltzer packet and drop it into a glass of water. Then she will drop an unopened Alka-Seltzer packet into the water. Watch the Alka-Seltzer for about a minute.

Discuss these questions:

- What insights about being open and transparent with others can you glean from this demonstration?

- What happens in our relationships when we're open and transparent with others? If possible, tell a story from your own experience.

- How do we build trust in our friendships to help us be more transparent?

Read John 12:44, 46 aloud:

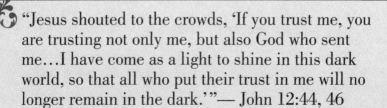

"Jesus shouted to the crowds, 'If you trust me, you are trusting not only me, but also God who sent me...I have come as a light to shine in this dark world, so that all who put their trust in me will no longer remain in the dark.'"— John 12:44, 46

Discuss this question as a group:

❧ **What role does trusting God play in coming out of the dark?**

When we trust others, we're more able to be open and vulnerable with them. The same is true of our relationship with God—the more we trust him, the more we can be open with him. And he can help us build trustworthy friendships.

Getting Real 🌀 —————————
(about 10 minutes)

We've already taken one step by opening up to each other. Now we're going to look at how we can take what we've learned and act on it this week. Look at the options below, and select the one you'd like to take on this week—or come up with one of your own!

When you've decided on a Getting Real action, share your choice with a partner and write what you plan to do in the space provided. Make plans right now to connect with your partner sometime in the next week to check in and encourage each other.

- ❧ I'll tell a trusted friend something he or she doesn't know about me.

- ❧ I'll practice direct communication and talk face to face with someone I've been struggling with.

- ❧ I'll meditate on Psalm 139:1-6, letting God know I want to be transparent with him.

- ❧ I'll reflect on times I hide my real self from others and God, and I'll pray about the times I pretend to be someone I'm not.

Because friendship with Jesus and others is a priority, I'm going to:

_____

_____

_____

Closing

Stand a little apart from everyone else in the group. Hold your palms face up and lift your face to heaven, in a posture of openness before God.

Listen as your hostess reads Psalm 139:1-6 aloud. Make it your prayer as you hear the words.

> "O Lord, you have examined my heart and know everything about me. You know when I sit down or stand up. You know my thoughts even when I'm far away. You see me when I travel and when I rest at home. You know everything I do. You know what I am going to say even before I say it, Lord. You go before me and follow me. You place your hand of blessing on my head. Such knowledge is too wonderful for me, too great for me to understand!"—Psalm 139:1-6

Continue to stand with eyes closed and hands outstretched.

We are already transparent before God—there is nothing hidden. There's one question, though, that remains. Do you trust God with this knowledge of yourself? Will you stand before him as you are, trusting him to treat you with gentle friendship and love? Or will you try to hide yourself from him or close yourself off from him? Pray silently about those questions.

After a few minutes, your hostess will close with a prayer, asking God to help you all trust God with your true selves.

Week Four

ᴥ Helpful Hints for the Hostess ᴥ

People were a bit self-conscious about adopting the prayer posture at first. But they soon turned their attention to God, and their self-consciousness melted away. How we hold ourselves physically can affect our attitude and emotions, so encourage everyone to be open to God in both attitude and stance.

ᴥ Recipe Options ᴥ

Today's get-together is about being transparent before Jesus and others. It's about trusting others enough to reveal our hidden selves. In each of today's options, there's something hidden that women will reveal when they dig into the food.

Easiest Option:
+ filled doughnuts
+ beverages

Serve a variety of doughnuts with fruit, cream, and custard fillings.

Easy+ Option:

* hidden snacks
* beverages

Purchase a variety of snacks, such as cookies, candies, popcorn, chips, or snack mix—whatever your group likes. Portion out the snacks, putting each serving into a paper lunch bag. Fold over the tops and either staple them shut or tie them with ribbon so that the women won't be able to see the snacks inside. Mix up all the bags—there shouldn't be anything on the bags indicating what's inside them. It's important that there are several different snacks and that no one knows which snack she chose until she opens her bag.

Make It a Meal:

* burritos with a variety of fillings, such as beans and rice, beef and beans, chili and chicken, and so on.
* burrito toppings, such as salsa, sour cream, and guacamole
* beverages

Make or purchase burritos that look the same on the outside but have a variety of fillings to be discovered when cut open. Part of the fun for this meal is that people won't know what's inside the burritos, so mix them up, put them all on one baking sheet, and serve them all on one platter.

Week Five

Getting Through the Tough Stuff

Work through the tough stuff with Jesus and others.

Key Verses: Ephesians 4:15 & Philippians 2:1-3

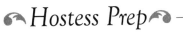 Hostess Prep

Today's snack is messy, so have napkins or wet wipes available.

You'll need:

☐ cheese puffs

☐ pens

☐ thick, wide rubber band (the largest one you can find)

☐ small rubber bands (1 for each person)

See the hostess helps on pages 59-61 for additional tips and other food ideas.

Getting to Know You

(about 15 minutes)

Enjoy getting to know all of your group members as you're waiting for everyone to arrive. While you chat, eat a snack provided by the hostess. Then begin your get-together with these discussion questions:

🍂 **What could the food we're eating today symbolize about friendship?**

🍂 **What things about friendship can be messy?**

Our food is messy and is sort of a challenge to eat. Today we're going to discuss the ways friendships are messy. We'll talk about how we get disappointed and how we disappoint others, and we'll explore how Jesus helps us be authentic and loving, even when it means saying the hard thing. Before we dive in, let's check in on the Getting Real challenges from last week.

Share with the entire group how you followed through with your commitment and what happened as a result.

Getting to Know God

(about 25 minutes)

Form pairs. Choose a scenario below, and practice what you'd say to a friend with your partner. Take turns choosing a scenario and practicing for 1 minute.

Q: Your friend broke a confidence and shared your secret. You found out. What will you say to your friend?

Q: You've just learned your friend has chosen a lifestyle you disagree with. How will you tell your friend your feelings?

Q: You just did something you know will hurt your friend deeply. How will you ask for forgiveness?

Discuss the experience with your partner:

Q: What do you think are healthy or unhealthy ways to handle disappointments and conflicts in a friendship?

Q: How is your relationship with Jesus messy sometimes?

Q: How is a messy human friendship like a messy relationship with God?

Read Ephesians 4:15 with your partner:

> "We will speak the truth in love, growing in every way more and more like Christ, who is the head of his body, the church."—Ephesians 4:15

Q: How can we hold to truth and love in messy friendships?

Q: How might saying the hard thing cause you to grow closer to others and Jesus?

After the discussion time with partners, form a circle with your entire group.

Your hostess will set a rubber band in the middle of the circle. Take turns grabbing hold of one side of it (it might be best to use two fingers) and describing a struggle or disappointment. The description doesn't have to be intimate—it should be vague and shouldn't use names—but the struggle should be something that's difficult to talk about and requires authenticity. For instance, you might say "I've been let down" or "I don't feel spiritually good enough." Don't let go of the rubber band, as the next person holds the rubber band and shares.

Eventually everyone will be holding the rubber band. Together, gently pull outward so that the rubber band stretches. Continue holding it like that (you can write notes afterward if you want) as you discuss these questions:

🍃 **How is this like or unlike the ways we are "stretched" in friendship?**

🍃 **How does Jesus challenge us to act when our friendships are stretched?**

Carefully let go of the rubber band, and turn to the same partner as before to discuss this question:

Q: Through which messy friendship or experience is Jesus stretching you? How will you respond?

Form another circle with your entire group, with everyone standing up. Hold hands with the women next to you. As you listen to the hostess, follow the instructions given if they apply to you.

Friendships can be fun, hopeful, and encouraging. But they're not always that way. Sometimes they're also disappointing, painful, and messy.

Sometimes we separate ourselves from each other and can't enjoy the love God intends for us. If you have ever been disappointed in a friendship or if you have disappointed someone, please let go of the hands you're holding and drop your arms to your sides.

Sometimes we say things that are harmful to others. I'd like anyone who's ever said something harmful to a friend to take a step backward.

Often we push others away. If anyone has ever pushed someone away or been pushed away, please take a step backward.

Sometimes we say something that's not true or don't say what needs to be said. We aren't authentic or loving in telling somebody the truth. If this has ever happened to you, I'd like you to turn and face away from the center of the circle.

Sometimes we pretend not to see the needs of other people. If there have been times you've ignored the needs of others and haven't reached out to them, please close your eyes and keep them closed.

We're meant to have close friendships, yet at times our struggles and disappointments keep us apart. If you've ever helped someone with a need or reached out to someone, I'd like you to turn around.

If you've ever taken the time to listen to a friend who was struggling, please take one step in.

If you've ever built someone up with encouraging words, open your eyes.

If you've ever shared a way that you failed someone, even though it was hard to say, take another step in.

God asks us to forgive one another. If you've ever forgiven someone, take the hands of the women next to you.

Then read aloud Philippians 2:1-3:

> "Is there any encouragement from belonging to Christ? Any comfort from his love? Any fellowship together in the Spirit? Are your hearts tender and compassionate? Then make me truly happy by agreeing wholeheartedly with each other, loving one another, and working together with one mind and purpose. Don't be selfish; don't try to impress others. Be humble, thinking of others as better than yourselves."—Philippians 2:1-3

Return to your seat, and take a few minutes to silently reflect on this passage and the experience you had with the group. Use the space provided to journal if you'd like to.

_____

_____

_____

_____

_____

_____

_____

_____

_____

Getting Real ✎ ──────────
(about 15 minutes)

We've already taken one step by reflecting on healthy friendships. Now we're going to look at how we can take what we've learned and act on it this week. Look at the options below, and select the one you'd like to take on this week—or come up with one of your own!

When you've decided on a Getting Real action, share your choice with a partner and write what you plan to do in the space provided. Make plans right now to connect with your partner sometime in the next week to check in and encourage each other.

- ✤ I'll invite a friend over to help me clean my garage, bedroom, closet, attic—anything that's a mess. While we're working together, we'll talk about how cleaning up a messy place is like or unlike cleaning up messy relationships.

- ✤ I'll write a letter to someone with whom I need to make amends. After praying about saying the right things, I'll call or meet that person and share what I wrote.

- ✤ I'll read Matthew 18:15-17 and confess the times I've failed to go directly to someone who has wronged me.

- ✤ I'll pray in front of a full wastebasket. I'll pray about the messy disappointments and hurts in my relationships.

Because friendship with Jesus and others is a priority, I'm going to:

_____

_____

_____

_____

_____

_____

_____

_____

_____

_____

_____

Closing

Friendships are messy, complicated, and sometimes painful. But they are precious gifts from God, and he uses them to stretch us and to bring us closer to Jesus.

Get a small rubber band from your hostess. Then think about a friendship in which loving the friend means you have to say a really hard thing. It may be Jesus or someone else in your life. Perhaps you need to confess something, or you may need to tell that person the truth in love. As you hold the rubber band, symbolizing how Jesus is working in your life, explore the friendship and the situation in prayer right now. Bring these to God, and ask that he would stretch you and guide you to be authentic and loving. Spend a few moments in silent prayer.

Your hostess will close with this prayer:

Jesus, thank you for stretching us and challenging us so that we might become more like you. We acknowledge that we contribute to our messy friendships by hurting and disappointing others and by sometimes not saying what should be said. Please help us not to run away but to go through friendships no matter what. Show us how to share truth in love, and make us truly authentic friends with you and with others. Amen.

Take home your rubber band, which symbolizes the ways Jesus helps you through tough situations. Use it as a tangible reminder to follow through on the Getting Real challenge.

Week Five

Helpful Hints for the Hostess

Here's an interesting point to bring up during this meal discussion: We wash up after eating messy foods, which is very much like clearing the air with friends. For example, if we eat something like Cajun Boil, we wash up because we don't want the stains and grime to pile up. Likewise, we clean up with friends so that other kinds of stains and grime don't pile up.

This exploration of messiness in friendship was timely for our group because everything we had discussed up to this point fit naturally into the idea of "messy" friendships. In your discussions today, encourage everyone to include and consider what you've talked about in previous weeks.

Extend the scenario discussion by exploring what a friend might do when saying the hard thing just isn't enough. Gather ideas and talk about practical ways someone might encourage a friend or tell the truth to a friend in a tough situation.

Don't worry if the rubber band breaks as everyone pulls on it; this will provide a great opportunity to talk about how Jesus uses friendships to ease our pain when we reach our own "breaking point." (After all, a snapped rubber band hurts a lot less with several people holding it rather than just one!)

Recipe Options

All of the food options today can be messy to eat. Relationships can be messy too! Today's food options will help women talk about how to handle the messy stuff that comes up in relationships all the time.

Easiest Option:
+ cheese puffs
+ beverages

Purchase bags of cheese puffs, and set them out for the group.

Easy+ Option:
- s'mores
- beverages

Purchase graham crackers, chocolate bars, and marshmallows. Marshmallows can be roasted in a fireplace, over the top of a stove, or can be melted in a microwave. (Make the s'more, put it on a plate, and put the whole thing in the microwave for 10-second intervals until it's all gooey.) Choose the option which works best for you.

You can go crazy with different kinds of candy bars, flavored marshmallows, and graham crackers in a variety of flavors, too. We recommend peanut butter cups instead of chocolate bars. Yum!

Make It a Meal:
- Cajun Boil
- beverages

This takes some effort—but it sure is delicious!

Make Cajun Boil using the following:

kielbasa (½ pound per person)
large, raw shrimp in the shell (½ pound per person)
small red potatoes (2 to 3 per person)
ears of corn (1 per person)
small onions (1 per person)
lemons (1 for every two people)
¾ cup Old Bay Seasoning
1 pound of butter
cocktail sauce
Dijon mustard

Bring six quarts of water to a boil. Add the Old Bay Seasoning. Cut the sausage into 2-inch pieces. Wash the potatoes, and cut them in half. Clean the corn, and break the cobs in half. Peel the onions, and cut them in quarters. Scrub the lemons, and cut them in quarters. Half an hour before everyone will arrive, put the sausage, corn, potatoes, onions, and lemons in the water, and boil for 20 minutes. While everything's boiling, put cocktail sauce and mustard into small bowls. Melt the butter, and pour it into several small bowls. When the potatoes are tender, rinse the shrimp, and add them to the pot. Gently stir. Turn off the heat.

Cover the table with one or two layers of butcher paper or paper tablecloths. Keep all the food in the kitchen until everyone has arrived and is seated at the table. After the meal has been prayed for, quickly drain the liquid from the pot. Careful! The steam can burn! Return the food to the pot, and take the pot to the dining table. Have all the participants lift up the edges of the tablecloth. Dump out the food in the middle of the table. No utensils are allowed! People eat with their hands, so provide lots of napkins—you may even want to provide wet washcloths at the end of the meal.

Week Six

Getting Committed

Explore the way Jesus' love helps us have committed friendships.

Key Verse: 2 Corinthians 5:14-15

Hostess Prep

Other than preparing the meeting space and providing food, there is no additional prep for this week. Celebrate the success of your weeks together!

You'll need:
- [ ] chewy candies
- [ ] pens
- [ ] 2 brooms
- [ ] 9-foot rope
- [ ] paper

See the hostess helps on pages 70 & 71 for additional tips and other food ideas.

Getting to Know You 🕊 ——————

(about 15 minutes)

Enjoy getting to know all of your group members as you're waiting for everyone to arrive. While you chat, eat a snack provided by the hostess. Then begin your get-together with these discussion questions:

🍂 **How would you describe today's food?**

🍂 **Tell about a friend who has stuck by you.**

Our food today sticks to us, and we're going to discuss how we can stick with others in friendship. We'll talk about Jesus' love and explore how we should be committed to God because God is committed to us. Before we dive in, let's check in on the Getting Real challenges from last week.

Share with the entire group how you followed through with your commitment and what happened as a result.

Getting to Know God 🕊 ——————

(about 25 minutes)

Decide on one person from your group to leave the room.

To avoid spoiling the surprise of this "Good and Evil" activity (so you know the person who has left the room didn't read ahead), turn to page 69 for the next set of instructions. Follow the instructions, and then call the missing group member back in. Give the person advice to find your object. It's entirely up to that woman to choose who to listen to.

After the woman has found an object, discuss with your group:

🍂 **What were you thinking as you went through this experience?**

🍂 **How is this experience like seeking God?**

Read Matthew 13:45-46 aloud:

> "Again, the Kingdom of Heaven is like a merchant on the lookout for choice pearls. When he discovered a pearl of great value, he sold everything he owned and bought it!"—Matthew 13:45-46

🌿 **How does this verse illustrate the way God searches for us?**

God searches for you like the merchant searches for a pearl. But God doesn't have distracting noises or messages—he hunts for you and finds you.

Find a partner, and read the passage below. Then discuss the questions that follow.

> "For this is what the Sovereign Lord says: I myself will search and find my sheep. I will be like a shepherd looking for his scattered flock. I will find my sheep and rescue them from all the places where they were scattered on that dark and cloudy day."—Ezekiel 34:11-12

Q: How have you seen God's commitment to find and rescue you?

Q: How is a commitment to another person like or unlike a commitment to God?

Get back together with the full group.

Two people in your group will hold two brooms about 20 inches apart. Your hostess will tie a 9-foot length of rope to one broom handle and loosely wrap the rope around both broom handles about three times.

Another person in your group will pull on the loose end of the rope as the first two volunteers try to keep the brooms apart.

Try the activity a few times so that everyone gets a chance to play.

After the activity, read 2 Corinthians 5:14-15 aloud:

"Either way, Christ's love controls us. Since we believe that Christ died for all, we also believe that we have all died to our old life. He died for everyone so that those who receive his new life will no longer live for themselves. Instead, they will live for Christ, who died and was raised for them." —2 Corinthians 5:14-15

💧 **How is what happened with the brooms like Jesus' love and commitment for us?**

Just as the rope pulled the brooms together, God's love pulls us into friendship with Jesus and others. The more we fall in love with Jesus, the more we want to do things his way and share his love with others. It's all about Jesus' commitment, power, and strength—not ours. And as we talked about earlier, our response to Jesus' love is automatic and natural.

Return to your partner. Read the Scripture below, and talk about the question that follows.

> "Jesus replied: '"You must love the Lord your God with all your heart, all your soul, and all your mind"...A second is equally important: "Love your neighbor as yourself."'"—Matthew 22:37, 39

Q: What does this verse teach you about friendships?

Getting Real
(about 10 minutes)

Gather with your entire group.

We've already taken one step by exploring how Jesus' love helps us have committed friendships. Now we're going to look at how we can take what we've learned and act on it this week. Look at the options below, and select the one you'd like to take on this week—or come up with one of your own!

When you've decided on a Getting Real action, share your choice with a partner and write what you plan to do in the space provided. Make plans right now to connect with your partner sometime in the next week to check in and encourage each other.

- ✦ I'll connect with a good friend and pray with him or her, asking God to help us both grow closer to Jesus and strengthen our commitment to him.

- ✦ With a friend, I'll compile a list of unnecessary human rules we've both been controlled by. We'll talk about the rules and then scribble through them and talk about how we'll live in Jesus' love and grace.

- ✦ Reflecting on how the Bible is God's love letter to us, I'll write a love letter to God as a prayer.

- ✦ I'll hold a cross and meditate on Galatians 2:20 as I commit my life to Christ, who gave his life for me.

Because friendship with Jesus and others is a priority, I'm going to:

_____

_____

_____

_____

Closing

Sit in a circle.

Get paper and a pen from your hostess, and write a prayer about friendship commitment. Your prayer could ask God for help in responding to his committed love and grace, confess a struggle or fear, or express the desire to listen only to God's messages and commit to them above all others.

After you've written your prayer, tear the paper into the shape of a cross and hold it to your chest, giving the prayer quietly and personally to God.

Then set your cross in the center of the circle, and work together with the entire group to make one big cross with your papers.

Think about Jesus' love as your hostess closes in prayer:

Jesus, your love brings us to you. Your kindness brings us to repentance. Your commitment to us leads us to glorify you. It's what you've made us for. Thanks for lavishing love, kindness, and grace upon us. Thank you for searching for us and finding us. Help us grow deeper in friendship with you, our best friend, and help us commit to sticking with others in friendship. Amen.

"Good and Evil" Activity Instructions

Here are the instructions for the "Good and Evil" activity during "Getting to Know God."

Hide a Bible (which will represent all that is good) on one end or side of the room, and hide a second object (something that represents all that is evil) on the opposite end or side of the room.

Everyone will be in one of two groups. Those whose birthdays are in January through July will help the person find the Bible. Those whose birthdays are in August through December will help the person find the "evil" object.

To help the person find their object, group members may use only the words *hotter* and *colder*.

Week Six

⌒ Helpful Hints for the Hostess ⌒

The people in our group really got into the "Good and Evil" activity, and it ended up being a powerful metaphor for real life. Participants will probably draw a lot of comparisons between this experience and what it's like to make choices in their faith and relationships when they hear so many other "voices" distracting them from what's good.

⌒ Recipe Options ⌒

All of today's food is sticky to help everyone understand the importance of sticking with Jesus and others.

Easiest Option:

+ caramels, gummy bears, taffy, and any other sticky candies
+ beverages

Choose the gooiest candies you can find!

Easy+ Option:

+ cinnamon rolls
+ beverages

Purchase gooey cinnamon rolls from your local grocery store or bakery, or bake them using your favorite recipe.

Make It a Meal:

✦ Sticky Chicken
✦ rice
✦ green salad

Make Sticky Chicken using the following:
chicken legs (1 per person)
chicken thighs (1 per person)
bacon (2 slices per person)
¾ cup maple syrup
¾ cup ketchup
½ cup apricot preserves
½ teaspoon ground cloves
1 tablespoon Worcestershire sauce
3 cloves garlic, crushed
1 tablespoon lemon juice

Wrap each chicken piece with a slice of bacon. Secure the bacon with a toothpick, and place the chicken in a baking pan. Mix together the maple syrup, ketchup, apricot preserves, cloves, Worcestershire sauce, garlic, and lemon juice in a small saucepan, and heat until well combined. Brush each chicken piece with the sauce, and bake at 400° F for about 45 minutes or until done.

Serve with rice and a salad.

Journal

Célébrons notre foi

Celebrate our Faith

Celebriamo la nostra fede

Uczcijmy naszą Wiarę

Papal Rose ™ Publishing

ISBN: 0-9691911-0-3
©1984 561448 Ontario Inc.
C.O.B. Papal Rose Publishing
303-177, rue Nepean Street, Ottawa, Canada K2P 0B4

"Célébrons notre foi"
L'édition deluxe officielle sous license exclusive de la Conférence des Evêques Catholique du Canada.

"Celebrate our Faith"
The official deluxe volume under exclusive license by the Canadian Conference of Catholic Bishops.

"Celebriamo la nostra fede"
Edizione ufficiale e di lusso soto autorizzazione esclusiva del Congresso Canadesi dei Vescovi Cattolici.

„Uczcijmy naszą Wiarę"
Oficjalne wydanie luksusowe z wyłącznymi prawami Kanadyjskiej Rady Biskupów Katolickich.

Joannes Paulus PP. II

Table des matières

Table of Content

Indice

Zawartość

Remerciements

Acknowledgement

Ringraziamento

Podziękowanie

ÉDITEUR / PUBLISHER / EDITORE / POSŁOWIE
Charles St. Clair Frazier

CONCEPTEUR / DESIGNER /
DISEGNATORE / PROJEKT ARTYSTYCZNY
Pierre J. Van Neste

DIRECTEUR DE LA PHOTOGRAPHIE /
DIRECTOR OF PHOTOGRAPHY /
DIRETTORE DI FOTOGRAFIA /
KIEROWNIK PRACOWNI FOTOGRAFICZNEJ
Allan de la Plante

PHOTOGRAPHE OFFICIEL DE LA VISITE DU PAPE /
OFFICIAL PAPAL TOUR PHOTOGRAPHER /
FOTOGRAFO UFFICIALE DELLA VISITA PAPALE /
OFFICJALNY FOTOGRAF PAPIESKIEJ WIZYTY
Murray Mosher

TEXTE / TEXT / TESTO / TEKST
Paul Delahanty

IMPRESSION ET GÉRANCE TECHNIQUE /
PRINTING AND TECHNICAL MANAGEMENT /
STAMPA E AMMINISTRAZIONE TÉCNICO /
DRUK I KIEROWNICTWO TECHNICZNE

K.G. Campbell Corporation

SÉPARATIONS COULEUR / COLOUR SEPARATION /
SEPARAZIONE CROMATICA / ORZSZCZEPIANIE
KOLOROW
TechnoCouleur Inc.

RELIURE / BINDING / LEGATURA / OKłADKA
T.H. Best Company Ltd.

PHOTOGRAPHES / PHOTOGRAPHERS /
FOTOGRAFI / AUTORZY ZDJĘĆ

Lorne Andras
Rob Beck
James B. Brawley
Bruce McDilda
Linda McLennan
Richard Morris
William Murenbeeld
Linda Lee Nicholls
François Proulx
Bill Wyshynski

PHOTO FEATURES LTD.

Carl Bigras
Jim Merrithew

DÉVELOPPEMENT DES PHOTOS /
PHOTO PROCESSING /
SVILUPPO FOTOGRAFICO / ZDJĘCIA

Profoto
Photo Features Ltd.

TRADUCTION / TRANSLATION /
TRADUZIONE / TŁUMACZENIE

Dr. Franco Ricci
Dr. Ireneuz Szarycz

FINANCES: ADMINISTRATION /
FINANCIAL: ADMINISTRATION /
FINANZIARIA: AMMINISTRAZIONE /
BUDŻET: ADMINISTRACJA

Gary E. Phomin

CONSEILLER JURIDIQUE/ LEGAL COUNSEL /
CONSIGLIERE LEGALE / RADCA PRAWNY

Ernest G. Tannis

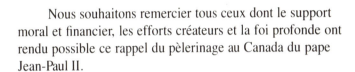

Nous souhaitons remercier tous ceux dont le support moral et financier, les efforts créateurs et la foi profonde ont rendu possible ce rappel du pèlerinage au Canada du pape Jean-Paul II.

We wish to thank all those whose moral and financial support, whose creative efforts, and whose deep faith made possible this reminder of the Canadian pilgrimage of Pope John Paul II.

Vogliamo ringraziare tutti coloro che con il loro sostegno morale, aiuto finanziario, sforzi creativi e fede profonda hanno reso possibile questa testimonianza del pellegrinaggio canadese di Papa Giovanni Paolo II.

Pragniemy podziękować tym wszystkim, których moralne i finansowe poparcie, twórcze wysiłki i głęboka wiara, umożliwiły wydanie tej pamiątki Kanadyjskiej Pielgrzymki Papieża Jana Pawła II.

Les voyages du pape Jean-Paul II à travers le monde ont servi d'inspiration à des millions de personnes. Où qu'il aille, il se mêle aux gens et leur parle leur propre langue, les incite à s'unir et exprime l'idéal chrétien de la réconciliation universelle. Son message s'adresse non seulement aux Chrétiens, mais aux adeptes de toutes les confessions.

Ce livre est dédié à Jean-Paul II, chef spirituel qui se donne sans compter à la cause de la paix et de la justice.

The travels of Pope John Paul II throughout the world have served as an inspiration to millions of people. Wherever he goes, he mingles with people and speaks to them in their own languages, fostering unity among them and expressing the Christian ideal of universal reconciliation. His dialogue is not only with Christians but reaches out to people of all faiths.

This book is dedicated to John Paul II, a spiritual leader who gives unselfishly of himself to the cause of peace and justice.

I viaggi di Papa Giovanni Paolo II per il mondo sono serviti da ispirazione a milioni di persone. Ovunque egli vada, si unisce ai popoli predicando nella loro lingua, promuovendo l'unità ed esprimendo gli ideali cristiani di riconciliazione universale. Il suo dialogo è diretto non solo ai Cristiani ma vuole raggiungere anche persone di altre fedi.

Questo libro è dedicato a Giovanni Paolo II, guida spirituale che dona se stesso altruisticamente alle cause della pace e della giustizia.

Podróże Papieża Jana Pawła II po całym świecie, służą jako inspiracja dla milionów ludzi. Gdziekolwiek jedzie, miesza się z tłumen i rozmawia z ludźmi w ich ojczystym języku, wzmacniając jedność między nimi i zaszczepiając chrześcijański ideał powszechnego pojednania. Słowa jego docierają nie tylko do Chrześcijan, lecz do ludzi wszystkich wyznań.

Książka ta poświęcona jest Janowi Pawłowi II, duchowemu przywódcy, który, bez cienia egoizmu, oddaje się sprawie pokoju i sprawiedliwości.

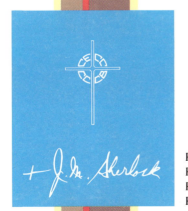

Président, Conférence des Evêques Catholique du Canada
President, Canadian Conference of Catholic Bishops
Presidènte, Congresso Canadesi dei Vescovi Cattolici
Prezydent, Konceja Kanadyjskiej rady Biskupòw Katolickich

. . . Que chante au Seigneur
la terre canadienne . . .

. . . May this Canadian land
sing to the Lord . . .

. . . Possa il Canada inalzare
un canto a Dio . . .

. . . Niech kanadyjska ziemia
w śpiewie wychwala Pana . . .

Introduction

Introduction

Introduzione

Wprowadzenie

Ce fut une célébration

Une célébration de vie, d'humanité, et surtout de foi.

Pendant un peu moins de deux semaines, il s'est déplacé parmi nous; il a parcouru plus de ce vaste territoire que n'en verront la plupart d'entre nous au cours de leur vie entière. La police, les hélicoptères et de grandes clameurs l'ont précédé. On a pu le voir parmi les fanions agités, les danseurs colorés, les reliquaires anciens et les autels flambants neufs; on l'a vu en papamobile au milieu des foules.

Nous nous souviendrons du contact d'une main.

Ce contact, en fait, ce fut celui d'un pape profondément humain, plein de chaleur, de compassion et d'humour. Nous avions le sentiment de le connaître ou, du moins, nous souhaitions le connaître. Nous désirions qu'il tourne la tête, qu'il nous regarde et nous adresse son sourire chaleureux, qu'il nous fasse signe. Nous l'avons considéré comme le pape du peuple, comme un personnage charismatique. Nous avons été émerveillés de son énergie, de la force qu'il puisait dans les autres, de sa disponibilité lorsqu'il s'arrêtait pour écouter et parler.

Dans un monde de faux héros et de prophètes contestables, Jean-Paul II fut vrai, non seulement en raison de sa personnalité, mais du fait qu'il représentait quelque chose de bien plus grand pour le Canada et le monde entier.

Les douze journées qu'il a passées parmi nous ont été longues et courtes à la fois. Mais son esprit et le message de sa visite resteront.

It was a celebration

A celebration of Life, of Humanity, and most particularly, of Faith.

For a little less than two weeks he moved among us, passing through more of this vast land than most people see in a lifetime. He was preceded by police and helicopters and great shouts. He was visible in the spectacle of waving flags and colourful dancers and old shrines and new and brilliant altars and the movement of the Popemobile through the crowds.

What we will remember is the touch of a hand.

It was the touch, in the end, of a very human Pope, one with warmth and compassion and humour. He was someone we felt we knew, or wanted to know. We wanted him to turn his head and look at us, to look at us with that warm smile, and to wave. We called him the People's Pope, a charismatic figure, a superstar. We marvelled at his energy, at the strength he drew from others, at his willingness to stop and to listen and to talk.

In a world of false heroes and questionable prophets, Pope John Paul II was, in the end, real, not just because of himself, but because he represented something far greater to Canada and to the World.

His twelve days here were long and very short. We will miss him. But the spirit and the message of his visit will remain.

È stata una celebrazione.

Una celebrazione della vita, dell'umanità ed in particolare della fede.

Per poco meno di due settimane ha vissuto fra di noi e ha visto di questo vasto paese molto di più di quanto la maggior parte delle persone ha la possibilità di vedere in tutta la vita. È stato accompagnato dalla polizia, da elicotteri, e da grida di esultanza. Si intravvedeva fra lo sventolio delle bandiere, fra i danzatori pittoreschi, vecchi santuari, altari nuovi e luminosi e attraverso i vetri della "Popemobile" che passava fra la folla.

Quello che ricorderemo è il tocco di una mano.

È stato il tocco, alla fine, di un Papa molto umano; un Papa con calore, compassione ed umorismo. È stato qualcuno che già ci sembrava di conoscere o che volevamo conoscere. Desideravamo che egli ci guardasse, che ci guardasse con quel suo sorriso caldo salutandoci. L'abbiamo chiamato il Papa del Popolo, una figura carismatica, una "superstar." Ci siamo meravigliati della sua energia, della Forza che traeva dagli altri, e del suo desiderio di soffermarsi ad ascoltarci e parlarci.

In un mondo di finti eroi e falsi profeti Papa Giovanni Paolo II è stato, alla fine, reale, non solo per la sua persona ma perchè ha rappresentato qualcosa di molto più grande per il Canada e per il mondo.

La sua visita, durata 12 giorni, è stata lunga ma nello stesso tempo molto breve. Ci mancherà. Il suo spirito e il messaggio della sua visita rimarranno con noi.

To był Triumf.

Triumf Życia, Ludzkości, a przede wszystkim, Wiary.

Był wśród nas niespełna dwa tygodnie, przemierzając w tym czasie więcej, niż niejeden widzi w przeciągu całego swego życia. Poprzedzany przez policję, helikoptery i głośne okrzyki, widzialny był na tle powiewających chorągiewek i barwnych tancerzy, starych sanktuariów i nowych wspaniałych ołtarzy. Widzialny był w Popemobilu, wolno posuwającym się przez tłumy.

Tym, co będziemy pamiętać, jest dotyk ręki.

Był to w końcu dotyk bardzo ludzkiego Papieża, pełnego ciepła i współczucia, Papieża z humorem. Był kimś, kogo zdawało się znamy, albo pragnęliśmy poznać. Chciało się, aby odwrócił głowę i spojrzał na nas, spojrzał na nas z tym ciepłym uśmiechem i pomachał do nas. Nazwaliśmy go Papieżem Ludzi, osobą o szczególnym darze łaski Bożej, gwiazdą. Podziwialiśmy jego energię, jego siłę, którą czerpał od innych, jego chęć zatrzymania się, aby posłuchać i porozmawiać.

W świecie fałszywych bohaterów i wątpliwych proroków, Papież Jan Paweł II był, nareszcie, realnym, prawdziwym i nie tylko z powodu swojej osobowości, lecz dlatego, że symbolizował coś dalece większego, zarówno dla Kanady, jak i dla Świata.

Dwanaście dni jego pobytu tutaj było zarazem długo i bardzo krótko. Będzie nam go brakowało. Lecz jego duch i posłannictwo jego wizyty pozostaną.

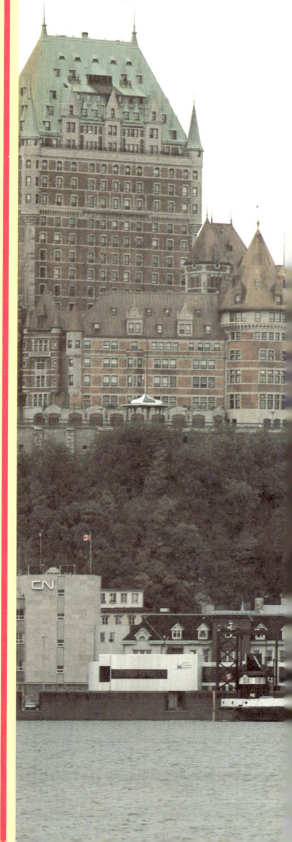

"Je viens vous dire
l'amour, la joie, les douleurs,
l'espérance de vos frères et de
vos soeurs de toutes les parties
du monde." Le Pape Jean-Paul II
vient comme "pasteur et frère",
et son message exprime "le
partage d'un frère dans la foi".

La célébration de cette foi
constitue le thème de la première
visite du Pape au Canada, et le
lien entre notre foi et notre
culture est le premier de ses
thèmes particuliers.

Foi et culture

Faith and Culture

Fede e Cultura

Wiara i Kultura

"I bring with me the love, the joy, the pain, and the hope of your brothers and sisters all over the world." Pope John Paul II comes as "pastor and brother," and his message is one of sharing, "of a brother in the faith".

The celebration of that faith is the theme of this first visit to Canada of a Pope, and the link between our faith and our culture, the first of his special themes.

At the place where the "church of Christ began to spread throughout North America" the

"Porto con me l'amore, la gioia, il dolore e la speranza dei vostri fratelli e sorelle di tutto il mondo." Papa Giovanni Paolo II viene come "pastore e fratello," e il suo messaggio di comunione è "di un fratello nella fede."

La celebrazione di quella fede è il tema di questa prima visita del Papa in Canada, e l'unione fra la nostra fede e la nostra cultura è il tema del suo primo messaggio.

Nel luogo ove la "Chiesa di Cristo incominciò a diffondersi nel Nord America" il Vescovo di Roma vuole "incontrarci ed unirsi a noi in questa professione di fede." Noi siamo tutti "pietre viventi" e Cristo la "prima pietra." La nostra fede è "un unione incredibile" e la sorgente della nostra forza.

„Przynoszę ze sobą miłość, radość, ból i nadzieję waszych braci i sióstr na całym świecie." Papież Jan Paweł II przyjeżdża jako „duszpasterz i brat," a jego posłannictwem jest dzielenie „brata w wierze."

Triumf Wiary jest tematem tej pierwszej podróży Papieża do Kanady, a więc między naszą wiarą i naszą kulturą jest pierwszym z jego specjalnych tematów.

W miejscu, skąd „Kościół Chrystusa zaczął rozprzestrzeniać się po Ameryce Północnej", Biskup Rzymu pragnie „spotkać się i połączyć razem w tym wyznaniu Wiary". Wszyscy jesteśmy „żyjącymi kamieniami", a Chrystus jest „fundamentem". Nasza Wiara jest „zadziwiającą jednością" i źródłem naszej siły.

Sur le site du "premier foyer de l'Église en Amérique du Nord", l'Évêque de Rome souhaite que "nous nous rencontrions et [que] nous nous unissions dans cette profession de foi". Nous tous sommes des "pierres vivantes" et le Christ est "la pierre fondamentale". Notre foi est une "surprenante unité", elle est aussi source de notre force.

Notre foi prend ses racines dans la culture qu'ont apporté avec eux nos fondateurs, enrichie par les autochtones, puis par les nouveaux immigrants. Elle fait partie de l'héritage que nous ont laissé les premiers explorateurs et les missionnaires. La culture qui s'est développée a ses origines dans les pays chrétiens d'Europe. Elle s'est consolidée et diversifiée à travers les siècles. Divers peuples l'ont enrichie – autochtones et immigrants. Chacun "a su conserver son identité en demeurant ouvert aux autres cultures".

Le lien entre foi et culture est fondamental pour l'avenir. Des formes anciennes du christianisme ont disparu, et la culture actuelle est ouverte à de nouveaux courants de pensée. Elle représente une grande promesse pour "les droits de l'homme, la paix, la justice, l'égalité, le partage, la liberté …", mais notre foi "devra apprendre à se dire et à se vivre".

Alors seulement saurons-nous "susciter une nouvelle culture, intégrer la modernité de l'Amérique sans renier sa profonde humanité".

Notre foi doit rester vivante et forte, elle doit être toujours plus personnelle, plus enracinée dans la prière et l'expérience des sacrements pour "qu'elle rejoigne le Dieu vivant".

Bishop of Rome wants to "meet and join together in this profession of Faith." We are all "living stones" and Christ the "foundation stone". Our faith is a "surprising unity" and a source of our strength.

Our faith is rooted in and linked with the culture brought by the original founders, and enriched by the Native peoples and later immigrants. It was part of the legacy of the first explorers and the religious missionaries and witnesses to the faith. The culture that developed was rooted in the Christian countries of Europe, and consolidated and diversified through the centuries. It has been enriched by diverse peoples – natives and immigrants – who "have succeeded in preserving their identity while remaining open to other cultures."

This link between faith and culture is fundamental to the future. Old forms of Christendom have gone and the new culture is open to new currents of thought. Its promise for the future of "human rights, for peace, justice, equality, sharing, freedom …" is great but we must learn to "articulate" our faith and "to live it."

Only then will we develop a "new culture that will integrate the modernity of America even while preserving its deep-seated humanity."

Our faith must remain active and strong, it must become always more personal, more and more rooted in prayer and in the experience of the sacraments in order to "reach the living God."

La nostra fede è radicata nella cultura dei fondatori originali, è stata arricchita dagli indigeni e più tardi dagli immigrati. È stata parte dell'eredità dei primi esploratori e dei missionari e testimoni della fede. La cultura che si è sviluppata aveva le sue radici nei paesi cristiani europei e si è consolidata e diversificata attraverso i secoli. È stata arricchita da diversi popoli … indigeni ed immigrati … che "sono riusciti a mantenere la loro identità pur rimanendo aperti ad altre culture."

Questo vincolo tra fede e cultura è fondamentale per il futuro. Le vecchie forme di Cristianesimo sono sparite e la cultura è aperta a nuovi sviluppi del pensiero. La promessa per un futuro di "diritti umani, pace, guistizia, ugualianza, comunione, libertà" è grande, ma dobbiamo imparare ad "articolare" la nostra fede ed "a viverla."

Solo allora si svilupperà "una nuova cultura che integrerà la modernità dell'America mantenendo la sua profonda umanità."

La nostra fede deve rimanere attiva e forte, deve diventare sempre più personale, sempre più radicata nella preghiera e nell'esperienza dei sacramenti in modo da "raggiungere il Dio vivente."

Nasza Wiara, zakorzeniona w kulturze jej założycieli, pozostając w ścisłym z nią związku, została wzbogacona przez rdzenną ludność, a następnie emigrantów. Była to część naszego spadku po pierwszych badaczach, misjonarzach i wyznawcach Wiary. Kultura, która się rozwinęła, wzięła swój początek z chrześcijańskich krajów europejskich, a utwierdzała się i wzbogacała w przeciągu wieków. Została wzbogacona przez różnych ludzi, tubylców i emigrantów, którym „udało się zachować własną tożsamość nie odgradzając się jednocześnie od innych kultur".

Ta łaczność między wiarą i kulturą ma istotne znaczenie dla przyszłości. Stare formy chrześcijaństwa przeminęły i nowa kultura stoi otworem dla nowych idei. Jej obietnice na przyszłość, dotyczące „praw człowieka, pokoju, sprawiedliwości, równości, podziału, wolności …" są ogromne, lecz musimy nauczyć się „jasno wyrażać" naszą wiarę i „żyć według jej przykazań."

Tylko wtedy rozwiniemy „nową kulturę, która dopełni nowoczesność Ameryki, a jednocześnie zachowa jej głęboko zakorzenioną humanitarność."

Nasza wiara musi pozostać żywą i silną, musi zawsze być bardziej osobistą, więcej i więcej opartą na modlitwie i duchowym uniesieniu, żeby dostąpić łaski „połączenia się z Bogiem."

... Nous inaugurons aujourd'hui
une fête destinée à avoir un grand
retentissement dans vos cœurs ...

... On this day we are beginning
a celebration to be long treasured
in your hearts ...

... In questo giorno iniziamo una celebrazione
che dovrà a lungo restare chiuso
nei vostri cuori ...

... Dzisiaj rozpoczynamy uroczystość, którą
długo, jak skarb, zachowacie
w sercach Waszych ...

... Il est très bon d'être avec vous ...

... It is very good to be with you ...

... È bello essere con voi ...

... Cieszę się, że jestem z Wami ...

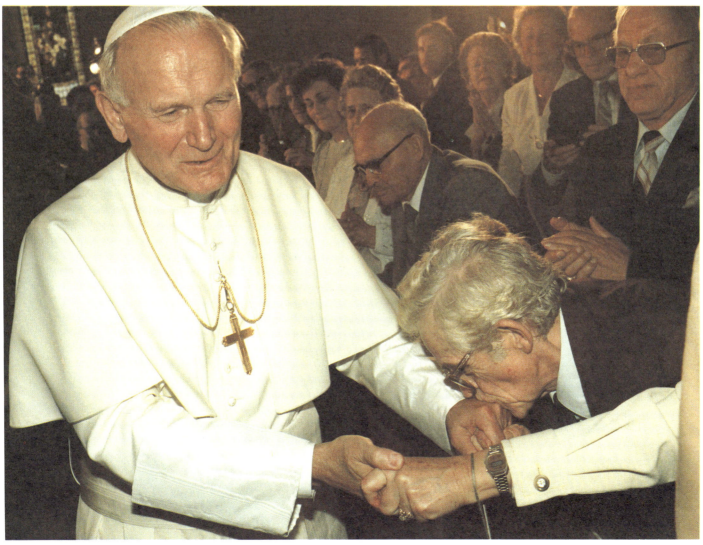

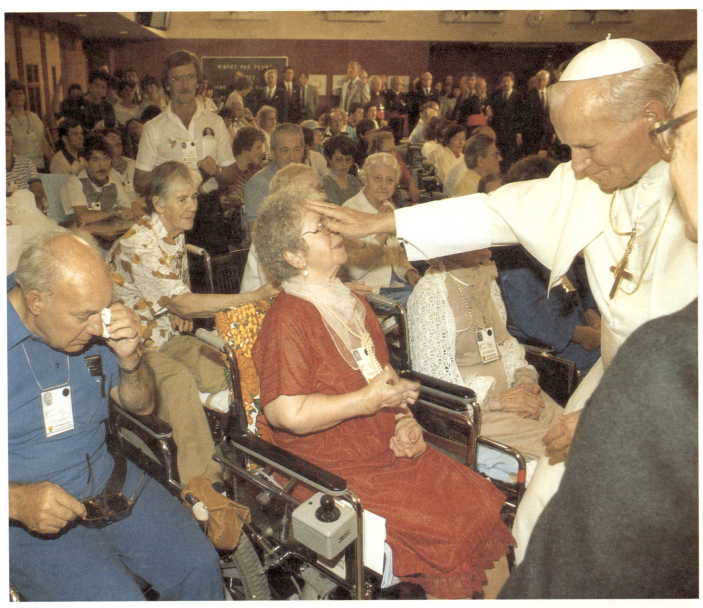

... Je suis parmi vous pour partager
le pain et la parole,
pour partager l'espérance ...

... I am among you to share the bread
and the word, to share hope ...

... Sono fra voi per dividere il pane
e la parola, per dividere la speranza ...

... Jestem wśród Was, aby dzielić
chleb i Słowo, dzielić nadzieję ...

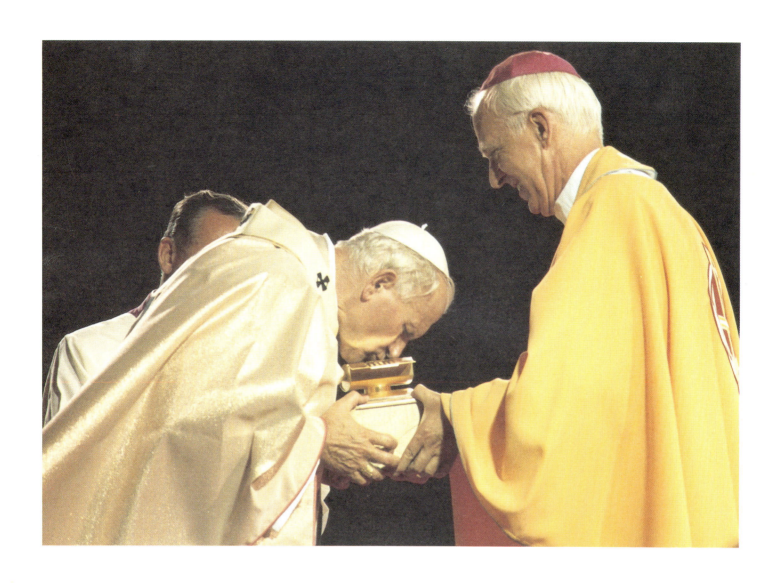

Marie

Mary

Maria

Maria

"Nous apprenons de Marie le secret de la joie qui vient de la foi, pour en illuminer notre vie et celle des autres." C'est ainsi que Jean-Paul II résume ce thème, sur l'emplacement de l'église la plus ancienne du Canada.

Les premiers colons étaient "des hommes de grande foi, consacrés à Notre-Dame". Et dans le monde entier, la dévotion à Marie est "fortement ancrée dans le coeur du peuple chrétien, dans sa prière quotidienne, dans les familles et dans les communautés paroissiales".

Cette dévotion a été grande du moment qu'il y a eu évangélisation. Elle est nécessaire, car nous ne pouvons "annoncer et réaliser l'oeuvre de son Fils sans regarder vers sa Mère, sans admirer sa disponibilité et sa foi".

"We learn from Mary the secret of the joy which comes from faith, in order to enlighten with it our lives and the lives of others." Thus Pope John Paul II sums up his theme at the site of the oldest church in Canada.

The early settlers were "people of great faith, consecrated to Our Lady." All over the world the devotion to Mary is "firmly anchored in the hearts of the Christian people, in their daily prayers, in their families and in their parishes."

This devotion has been strong as long as there has been evangelization. It is necessary because we cannot "announce and realize the Son's work without turning to the Mother, without admiring her openness and her faith."

"Impariamo da Maria il segreto della gioia che viene dalla fede, in modo che questo illumini la nostra vita e quella degli altri." Così Papa Giovanni Paolo II riassume il suo discorso nella più vecchia chiesa canadese.

I primi pionieri erano "persone di grande fede devoti alla Madonna." In tutto il mondo la devozione a Maria è "saldamente ancorata nei cuori dei popoli cristiani, nelle loro preghiere giornaliere, nelle loro famiglie e nelle loro parrocchie."

Questa devozione ha perseverato fino a che c'è stata l'evangelizzazione. Inoltre è necessaria perché non si può "annunciare e realizzare l'opera del Figlio senza rivolgersi alla Madre e senza ammirarne la Sua bontà e la fede."

„Uczymy się od Maryi sekretu radości, który wypływa z wiary, żeby oświetlić nim nasze życie i życie innych." W ten sposób Papież Jan Paweł II podsumowuje swoje przemówienie przed najstarszym kościołem w Kanadzie.

Pierwsi osadnicy byli „ludźmi głębokiej wiary, całkowicie oddanymi Najświętszej Pannie." Na całym świecie pacierz do Najświętszej Panny jest mocno zakorzeniony w sercach chrześcijan, w ich codziennych modlitwach, w ich rodzinach i parafiach.

Modlitwa ta zajmuje trwałą pozycję tak długo, jak długo istnieje wyznawanie wiary. I to jest konieczne, ponieważ nie możemy „głosić i urzeczywistniać trudu Syna, bez zwracania się do Jego Matki, bez uwielbiania Jej szczerości, Jej wiary.

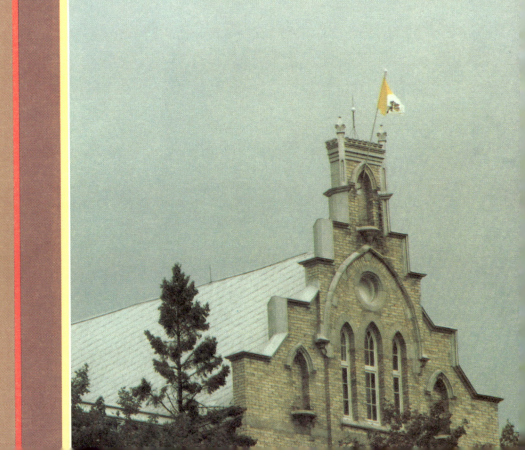

... Vous venez ici en pèlerins ...

... You come here as pilgrims ...

... Venite da pellegrini ...

... Przychodzicie tutaj
jako pielgrzymi ...

C'est ainsi que des sanctuaires mariaux ont été érigés. Les pèlerins s'y rendent, et "la Vierge elle-même y montre sa tendresse" à sa manière propre. Ces moments de pèlerinage devraient être "des temps forts de la vie chrétienne", car "ce sont des occasions de ressourcement" et de renouvellement.

Marie a cru avant tous les autres "au mystère du Christ, et elle a sa part, une part suréminente, dans la Foi et l'Espérance de l'église". Elle est "le modèle primordial de l'Église qui chemine sur la voie de la foi, de l'espérance [...] et de la charité".

Marie a contribué "à construire la foi du peuple de Dieu au cours de nombreuses générations". Et l'Église qui est sur cette terre exulte de joie en professant "sa participation à la foi de Marie".

It has led to the building of special Marian shrines where pilgrims come and where the "Virgin herself shows her tenderness" in a special way. And such pilgrimages should be "high points in the Christian life" because they are opportunities for a "return to the sources" and for renewal.

Mary was the "first to believe" in the mystery of Christ, and she has "a most eminent part, in the faith and hope of the Church." She is the "primordial model for the Church as it makes its way along the path of faith, hope and charity."

Mary helped "to build the faith of the people of God over many generations." And the Church on earth rejoices in professing "its participation in Mary's faith."

Essa ha condotto alla edificazione di santuari dedicati alla Madonna dove i pellegrini si recano e dove "la Vergine stessa mostra la sua tenerezza" in modo particolare. Tali pellegrinaggi dovrebbero essere "mete importanti nella vita cristiana" perché sono opportunità per "un ritorno alle origini" e per un rinnovamento.

Maria fu "la prima a credere" nel mistero di Cristo, ed ha "un ruolo eminente nella fede e nella speranza della Chiesa." È il "modello primordiale della Chiesa mentre questa procede lungo il sentiero della fede, della speranza e della carità."

Maria aiutò a "costruire la fede del popolo di Dio per molte generazioni." E la Chiesa terrena gioisce professando "la sua partecipazione alla fede di Maria."

Stało się to bezpośrednią przyczyną wznoszenia Maryjnych kaplic, które przyciągają rzesze pielgrzymów, gdzie w swoisty sposób „Niepokalana okazuje swoją dobroć." Takie pielgrzymki powinny zajmować „szczególną pozycję w chrześcijańskim życiu", gdyż są one szansą „powrotu do źródła", szansą odnowy.

Maryja Panna była „pierwszą, która uwierzyła" w tajemnicę Chrystusa i grała „najwybitniejszą rolę w wierze i nadziei Kościoła". Jest ona odwiecznym modelem dla Kościoła, w jego drodze do celu ścieżką wiary, nadziei i miłosierdzia.

Maryja wspomagała „rozwijać wiarę człowieka Bożego przez wiele generacji." A Kościół na ziemi raduje się, głosząc „swój udział w wierze Maryi."

... La renaissance de la culture indienne sera la renaissance des vraies valeurs dont elle a hérité et qu'elle a préservées ...

... The revival of Indian culture will be a revival of those true values which they have inherited and safeguarded ...

... La rinascita della cultura indiana sarà il rinnovo de quei veri valori che gli indiani hanno ereditato e protetto ...

... Odrodzenie kultury Indian, będzie odrodzeniem tych prawsziwych wartości, które oni odziedziczyli i chronili ...

29

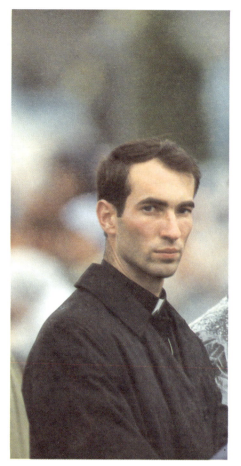

... Le secret de la joie
qui vient de la foi ...

... The secret of the joy
which comes from faith ...

... il segreto della gioia
che viene dalla fede ...

... tajemnica radości,
która wypływa z wiary ...

Le mystère de Dieu

Mystery of God

Mistero di Dio

Tajemnica Boża

"Cette terre est sainte, car Dieu l'habite, et son mystère demeure comme une lumière, comme un appel, comme une force, au coeur de chaque personne humaine, qui s'ouvre à la volonté de Dieu." Le Pape Jean-Paul II nous rappelle que le mystère de Dieu est toujours présent dans le monde.

"Dieu s'est fait homme en Jésus-Christ, pour que chaque homme laisse pénétrer en lui la lumière et l'amour de Dieu."

Cette présence de Dieu au monde fut autrefois plus manifeste, mais à l'époque actuelle, elle semble parfois faire défaut. Il se peut que nous l'oublions pendant un temps, mais "le coeur humain ne s'habitue pourtant pas" à cette absence.

"This land is holy because God dwells in it; his mystery remains as a light, as a call, as a force in the heart of every human person who remains open to his will." Pope John Paul II reminds us that the mystery of God is ever present in the world.

"God became man in Jesus Christ so that each and every human person might be imbued with the light and the love of God."

This presence of God in the world once seemed more evident, but in modern times he sometimes seems to be missing. We may forget him for a time, but "for the human heart" there is "no way to become accustomed" to his absence.

"Questa terra è santa perché Dio vi abita; il Suo mistero rimane come luce, voce, forza nel cuore di ogni essere umano che si apre alla Sua volontà" Papa Giovanni Paolo II ci ricorda che il Mistero di Dio è sempre presente nel mondo.

"Dio si fa uomo in gesù Cristo in modo che ogni essere umano sia impregnato della luce e dell' amore di Dio."

Un tempo la presenza di Dio nel mondo sembrava più viva, ma nei tempi moderni pare mancare. Possiamo dimenticarlo momentaneamente ma "per il cuore umano non c'è modo di abituarsi" alla sua assenza.

Per l'uomo la ricerca della felicità è continua, ma il tentativo di attenuare il bisogno di Dio con altre cose non ci soddisfa e ritroviamo "un nuovo

"Ta ziemia Świetą jest, gdyż Bóg tutaj mieszka, Jego tajemnica jest lekką, jak zawołanie, jak moc w sercu każdej istoty ludzkiej, która poddaje się Jego woli." Papież Jan Paweł II przypomina nam, o nieustannej obecności Tajemnicy Bożej na świecie.

"Bóg stał się człowiekiem w Jezusie Chrystusie, żeby każdy bez wyjątku, mógł nasycić się światłością i miłością Bożą."

Niegdyś obecność Boga na świecie wydawała się bardziej oczywistą, lecz w obecnych czasach wydaje sie, że go czasami brakuje. Możemy zapomnieć o nim na jakiś czas, lecz "serce ludzkie nigdy nie przyzwyczai się" do Jego nieobecności.

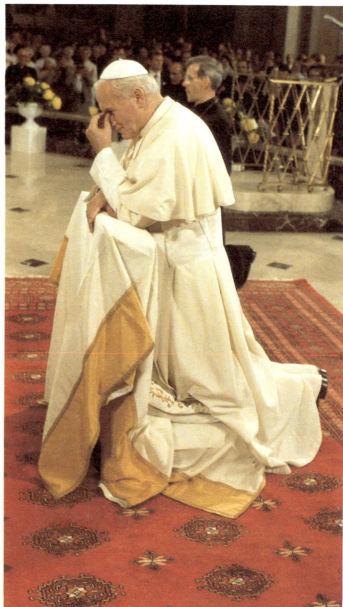

La quête du bonheur est permanente chez l'homme, mais tenter d'étancher la soif que nous avons de Dieu par autre chose ne nous satisfait pas, et nous ressentons alors une nouvelle "faim du spirituel". En conséquence, l'apparente absence de Dieu dans le désert de notre monde moderne "peut devenir le temps de la redécouverte de Dieu". Et ce temps n'est pas loin de nous.

Nous avons tous fait, un jour ou l'autre, des "expériences de lumière et de paix". "Les occasions" de cette mystérieuse présence de Dieu "sont multiples". "La naissance si merveilleuse d'un enfant, le début d'un amour authentique, la confrontation à la mort d'un proche, à l'échec ou au mystère du mal, la compassion pour la misère d'autrui, la grâce d'avoir échappé à un accident ou d'être guéri d'une maladie, la création d'une oeuvre d'art, la contemplation silencieuse de la nature, la rencontre d'une personne habitée par Dieu, la participation à une communauté priante : autant d'étincelles qui éclairent la route vers Dieu, autant d'événements qui ouvrent la porte sur Dieu."

Mais lorsque la porte s'ouvre, la révélation elle-même vient de Dieu, du coeur du buisson ardent. Et comme Moïse, nous devons apprendre par la Parole, par la prière et la méditation, par l'Histoire sainte, ce qui constitue la "réalité absolument unique" de Dieu.

"Dieu est au-dessus de toute créature. Il est transcendance absolue. Là où s'achève le témoignage de la création, là commence la Parole de Dieu", et là nous apprenons le plus grand mystère : Dieu "est au-dessus de toute créature, qui est absolue transcendance, Dieu est devenu créature-homme." Ainsi donc, "les hommes–nés des hommes–naissent de Dieu."

The search for happiness is a continuing one for the human person. But trying to fill the hunger for God with other things does not satisfy us, and we then find a new "hunger for things spiritual." As a result the current, seeming absence of God in the desert of the modern world "may become the time of the rediscovery of God." And he is not far from us.

We all have known, at various times, "experiences of light and peace". God's mysterious presence "can be felt on occasions of all kinds". The "wondrous birth of a child, the beginning of authentic love, the meeting with death in the case of loved ones, the confrontation with failure or the mystery of evil, compassion felt for the sufferings of others, the grace of having escaped an accident or of recovering from a sickness, the creation of a work of art, the silent contemplation of nature, the meeting with a person in whom God dwells, participation in a praying community … All these are sparks which light up the road to God, events which open the door to God."

But when the door opens, revelation itself comes from God, from the heart of the burning bush. And as Moses did, we must learn through the Word, through prayer and meditation, through sacred history, what constitutes God's "absolutely unique reality."

God is "above every creature; he is absolute transcendence." And where the evidence of creation ends, "there begins the Word of God" and there we learn the greater mystery, that "God who is above all creatures, who is absolute transcendence, God has become a creature, a man." Thus, human beings, "born of human beings, are born of God."

bisogno per cose spirituali." Allora l'apparente assenza di Dio nel deserto del mondo moderno "può diventare il momento della Sua riscoperta." E lui non è lontano da noi.

Abbiamo tutti conosciuto in vari momenti "esperienze di luce e pace". La misteriosa presenza divina "può essere sentita nelle più diverse occasioni. La nascita miracolosa di un bambino, l'inizio dell'amore autentico, la morte dei cari, il confronto con la sconfitta o il mistero del male, la compassione provata per la sofferenza degli altri, la grazia di avere evitato un incidente o di guarire da una malattia, la creazione di un'opera d'arte, la silenziosa contemplazione della natura, l'incontro con una persona in cui risiede Dio, la comunione con una comunità in preghiera … sono scintille che illuminano la strada verso Dio, sono eventi che aprono la porta a Lui."

Ma quando la porta si apre la rivelazione viene da Dio, dal cuore del roveto ardente. Como fece Mosè, dobbiamo imparare attraverso la Parola, la preghiera, la meditazione, e la storia sacra cosa costituisce "la realtà unica ed assoluta di Dio."

Dio è "al di sopra di ogni creatura; è una trascendenza assoluta." Dove l'evidenza della creazione finisce, "lì incomincia la parola di Dio" e lì conosciamo il più grande dei misteri, cioè: "Dio che è al disopra di tutte le creature, che è trascendenza assoluta, Dio si è fatto uomo." Perciò, gli esseri umani, "nati da esseri umani sono nati da Dio."

Poszukiwanie szczęścia, jest niekończącym się procesem dla istoty ludzkiej. Próby zaspokojenia głodu Boga innymi drogami, nie zadowolają nas i odczuwamy nowy „głód duchowy". Jako rezultat nieobecności Boga w pustyni współczesnego świata „może nadejść czas odkrycia Boga na nowo". A On jest blisko nas.

Wszyscy doznaliśmy, w różnych okresach, „uczucia światła i spokoju". Tajemniczą obecność Boga „możemy odczuć przy różnych okazjach". „Cudowne narodziny dziecka, początek autentycznej miłości, śmierć osób bliskich, konfrontacja z porażką lub złymi siłami, współczucie cierpiącym, łaska uniknięcia wypadku lub uzdrowienia, tworzenie dzieła sztuki, rozmyślanie nad przyrodą, spotkanie z człowiekiem, w którym zamieszkał Bóg, udział we wspólnych modlitwach … Wszystko to są iskry, które oświetlają drogę do Boga, wydarzenia, które otwierają do Niego drzwi".Lecz gdy drzwi się otwieraja, następuje Boskie objawienie w postaci płonącego krzaka. Tak, jak uczynił Mojżesz, musimy, poprzez Słowo, poprzez modlitwę i medytację, poprzez najświętszą historię, poznać, co stanowi Boską, „bezwzględnie unikalną realność".

Bóg jest „ponad wszystkimi", jest On nadzmysłowym absolutem. „Tam, gdzie świadectwo stworzenia kończy się," tam rozpoczyna się Słowo Boże" i tam poznajemy najwspanialszą tajemnicę, że „Bóg, który jest ponad wszystkimi, nadzmysłowyn absolutem, stał się istotą, człowiekiem." A więc, człowiek, „zrodzony z człowieka, zrodzony jest z Boga".

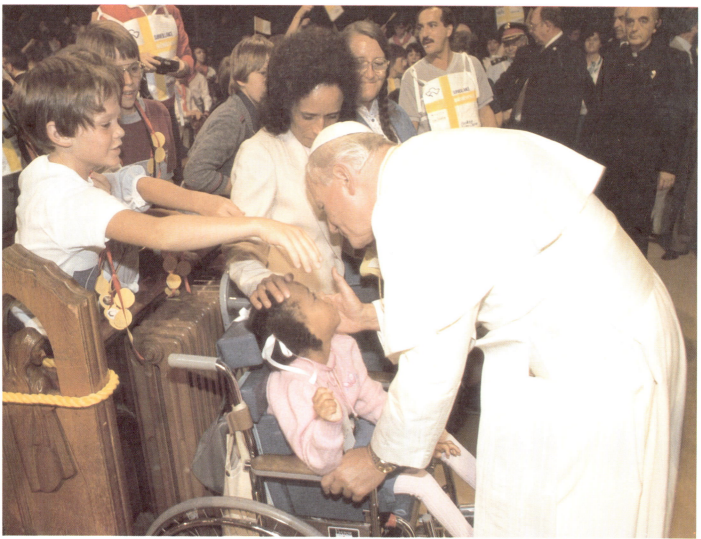

... Vivre comme des frères,
comme des amis ...

... live like brothers and sisters,
like friends ...

... vivete da fratelli e sorelle,
da amici ...

... żyjcie jak bracia i siostry,
jak przyjaciele ...

45

... Vous êtes heureux d'être tout près
   du Pape! Eh bien, le Pape aussi
   est très heureux d'être
   au milieu de vous!...

... You are happy to be so close
   to the Pope! Well, I can assure you
   that the Pope is also very happy
   to be among you!...

... Voi siete felici di essere vicini
   al Papa! Bene, posso assicurarvi
   che anche il Papa è felice
   di stare vicino a voi!...

... Radujecie się, że jesteście
   w pobliżu Papieża! Dobrze, mogę
   Was zapewnić, że Papież również bardzo
   się cieszy, że jest wśród Was ...

La famille

Family

Famiglia

Rodzina

"Puissent toutes les familles chrétiennes du monde, et nous tous, remplir notre vocation chrétienne, chacun conformément aux dons que nous avons reçus." Le Pape Jean-Paul II parle souvent du rôle de la famille et de l'intérêt qu'il lui porte.

L'amour que les époux chrétiens se portent l'un à l'autre est "une image toute spéciale de l'amour de Dieu", et les familles prennent "une part active à la mission de l'Église". De nombreuses familles, par leur exemple et leur enseignement, préservent et expliquent "la sainteté et l'unité de la famille" et contribuent à enseigner aux autres le message chrétien.

"May all the Christian families of the world, and all of us, fulfil our Christian vocation, each one in accordance with the gift we have received." Pope John Paul II speaks often of the role of the family and his concern for it.

The love between Christian spouses is an "altogether special image of God's love," and families "share actively in the mission of the Church." Many families, by their example and teaching, "uphold and explain the sanctity and unity of the family" and help aid in educating others to the Christian message.

"Possano tutte le famiglie cristiane e noi con loro, realizzare la nostra vocazione cristiana, ognuno in armonia col dono ricevuto." Papa Giovanni Paolo II parla spesso del ruolo della famiglia e della sua preoccupazione per essa.

L'amore tra coniugi cristiani è "un'immagine speciale dell'amore divino," e le famiglie partecipano attivamente nella missione della Chiesa. Molte famiglie, con il loro esempio ed insegnamento, "mantengono e spiegano la santità e l'unione della famiglia," ed aiutano ad educare gli altri al messaggio cristiano.

Wszystkie Rodziny chrześcijańskie całego swiata i my wszyscy, wypełnijmy swój chrześcijański obowiązek, każdy swój, w zależności od daru, jaki otrzymaliśmy. Papież Jan Paweł II często mówi o roli rodziny i swojej trosce o nią.

Miłość pomiędzy chrześcijańskimi nałżonkami, jest „osobliwym odbiciem miłości Bożej". Rodziny „biorą aktywny udział w misji Kościoła". Wiele rodzin, poprzez przykład i nauki, „podtrzymuje i wyjaśnia świętość i jedność rodziny" oraz wspomaga innych w nauczaniu misji chrześcijańskiej.

Nous devons une action de grâces particulière à Dieu pour les qualités de nos familles chrétiennes : leur fidélité réciproque, leur accueil de la vie, le service rendu aux autres par l'éducation de leurs enfants, leur témoignage, la préparation des jeunes à la maturité, la transmission du message évangélique dans les foyers chrétiens et dans la communauté.

Les familles ont trouvé de nombreuses occasions, tout au long de l'histoire de ce pays, de participer à l'élaboration de la culture et de la civilisation que nous connaissons ici, et ont vécu dans la liberté et l'espérance.

La vie moderne a engendré des incertitudes dans le monde, des difficultés économiques et des problèmes qui perturbent la structure sociale de la communauté. Mais par des décisions courageuses, les familles sont à même de donner au monde "un témoignage spécial". "L'amour éternel et indéfectible de Dieu s'exprime dans le pacte indissoluble de leur propre mariage sacramentel."

Les parents ont la "responsabilité particulière" d'aider à préparer les jeunes à leur rôle dans la vie. Mais "un dur labeur allié à un sens profond de la famille et de la communauté vous ont toujours soutenus dans la poursuite de votre idéal chrétien" et continueront à soutenir vos familles à l'avenir.

Les familles prennent "une part active à la mission de l'Église, en tant que communauté croyante et évangélisatrice et en tant que communauté en dialogue avec Dieu et au service de l'homme".

We owe special thanksgiving to God for the qualities of Christian families: their mutual fidelity, their openness to life, their service to others through educating their children, through witness, through the preparation of young people for maturity, through transmission of the Gospel message in Christian homes and in the community.

Families in this country have found many opportunities to participate in its history and the building of the culture and civilization here, and have lived in freedom and in hope.

Modern life has created uncertainties in the world, economic difficulties, and difficulties for families which disturb the social fabric of the community. But by "courageous decisions" families are able to give a "special witness" to the world. "God's everlasting and unbreakable love is expressed in the indissoluble covenant of their own sacramental marriage."

Parents have a "special responsibility" to help prepare young people for their roles in life. But "hard work and a strong sense of family and community have sustained you in the past in your upright Christian lives" and will continue to sustain families in the future.

Families "share actively in the mission of the Church, as a believing and evangelizing community and as a community in dialogue with God in the service of man."

Dobbiamo uno speciale ringraziamento a Dio per le qualità delle famiglie cristiane: la fedeltà reciproca, l'apertura verso la vita, il servizio fornito agli altri attraverso l'educazione dei figli, la testimonianza della fede, la preparazione dei giovani alla maturità, la comunicazione del messaggio evangelico nelle case cristiane e nella comunità.

Le famiglie hanno trovato molte opportunità nella storia di questo paese per costruirne la cultura e la civiltà, ed hanno vissuto in libertà e speranza.

La vita moderna ha creato nel mondo incertezze, difficoltà economiche e problemi che disturbano la struttura sociale della comunità. Ma con "coraggiose decisioni" le famiglie sono state capaci di fornire "una testimonianza speciale" al mondo. "L'amore eterno ed indistruttibile di Dio è espresso nel patto indissolubile del sacramento del matrimonio."

I genitori hanno una "responsabilità speciale" nel preparare i giovani al loro ruolo nella vita. Ma "il duro lavoro ed il forte senso della famiglia e della comunità vi hanno sostenuto nel passato nella vostra retta vita cristiana" e continueranno a sostenere le famiglie nel futuro.

Le famiglie "partecipano attivamente nella missione della Chiesa come comunità credente ed evangelica e come comunità in dialogo con Dio al servizio del l'uomo."

Winni jesteśmy Bogu szczególne podziękowanie za przymioty, jakimi obdarzone zostały rodziny chrześcijańskie. Ich obopólna wierność, szczerość życiowa, ich usługi dla innych poprzez kształcenie dzieci, poprzez przygotowanie młodzieży do wieku dojrzałego, poprzez rozpowszechnianie nauk Ewangelii w domach chrześcijańskich i w różnych środowiskach.

W historii tego kraju rodziny znajdowały wiele możliwości do szerzenia kultury i cywilizacji oraz do życia w nadziei i wolności.

Współczesny świat pełen jest niepewności, problemów ekonomicznych oraz problemów, tkóre zakłóciły socjalną strukturę społeczeństwa. Lecz dzięki „odważnym decyzjom", rodziny są w stanie przedstawić światu „szczególny dowód". „Wieczna i nieniszczalna miłość Boska, jest wyrażona w nierozerwalnym zobowiązaniu ich własnego Sakramentu małżeńskiego".

Rodzice mają „szczególny obowiązek" pomocy w przygotowaniu młodzieży do jej życiowej roli. Lecz „ciężka praca i silne poczucie odpowiedzialności za rodzinę i środowisko, podtrzymały Was i nie pozwoliły zboczyć z drogi chrześcijańskiego życia" i będą podtrzymywać Was w przyszłości.

Rodziny „biorą aktywny udział w misji Kościoła, jako wierząca i głosząca ewangelię społeczność oraz, jako społeczność w dialogu z Bogiem, na służbie u człowieka."

... Nous rendons grâce
pour notre vocation chrétienne ...

... We give thanks for our
Christian vocation ...

... Rendiamo grazie
per la nostra vocazione cristiana ...

... Dziękujemy Bogu za nasze
chrześcijańskie powołanie ...

"Je vous encourage à former des communautés humaines exemplaires par leur pratique de la solidarité." Le Pape Jean-Paul II nous invite également à former "un peuple chrétien, des communautés chrétiennes dignes de ce nom".

La "communauté chrétienne" est le "signe de la présence de Dieu dans le monde". Les communautés paroissiales et les autres communautés devraient réaliser un programme de témoignage du Christ, de charité et de recherche de la justice. Les communautés ecclésiales devraient garder "la dignité que leur donne le Christ".

Les communautés

Community

Comunità

Społeczność

"I encourage you to form human communities that will be examples in their practice of solidarity." Pope John Paul II also calls on us to form "a Christian people, Christian communities worthy of the name."

The "Christian community" is a "sign of the presence of God in the world." Parishes and various communities should carry out a program of witness to Christ, charity, and a seeking after justice. And Church communities should maintain "the dignity vested in them by Christ."

"Vi incoraggio a formare comunità umane, che saranno esempi di pratica di solidarietà." Papa Giovanni Paolo II ci invita anche a formare "un popolo cristiano, delle comunità cristiane degne di tale nome."

La "comunità cristiana" è un "segno della presenza di Dio nel mondo." Le parrocchie e le varie comunità dovrebbero svolgere un attività di testimonianza di Cristo, di carità, e di ricerca di giustizia. E le comunità ecclesiastiche dovrebbero mantenere "la dignità di cui Cristo le ha investite."

„Zachęcam Was do organizowania społeczności, które będą przykładem praktycznej solidarności". Papież Jan Paweł II wzywa nas również do formowania „społeczności chrześcijańskich, które godne byłyby tej nazwy".

„Chrześcijańska Społeczność", jest „znakiem obecności Boga na świecie". Parafie oraz różne społeczności, powinny propagować wiarę w Chrystusa, miłosierdzie, poszukiwanie prawdy. Natomiast środowiska kościelne, powinny zachować „godność nadaną im przez Chrystusa".

Le don de la grâce, la foi, la prière et le pouvoir des sacrements sont nécessaires à la vie chrétienne, mais il faut y ajouter la charité et "l'amour du prochain". Cet amour est "réconciliation". Il est aussi "volonté d'unité et de fraternité". Cet amour est respect et accueil du pauvre, "recherche de ce qui est utile au prochain", non seulement des besoins matériels, mais du zèle missionnaire.

L'esprit communautaire de notre pays "subit une transformation profonde". La vie urbaine, les crises économiques, et une crise spirituelle – crise des valeurs – atteignent les communautés locales. Mais nous pouvons "regarder l'avenir avec sérénité" si nous demeurons fermes dans la foi et si nous laissons l'esprit du Christ trouver "les réponses aux nouveaux défis". Nous devrions nous montrer "solidaires" et accepter "d'être le levain dans l'Église et dans la société".

La foi aidera nos communautés à relever ces nouveaux défis. Le partage, la justice et la charité doivent s'enraciner "dans le ressourcement spirituel". Nous devons "vivifier la foi" pour qu'elle entraîne tous les engagements de charité : respect des personnes, respect des droits de l'homme et respect de la vie, refus de la violence, souci des catégories moins favorisées et institution de mesures sociales pour plus d'égalité et de justice, zèle missionnaire et volonté de simplicité et de partage.

Il faut ouvrir nos communautés "à l'esprit du Christ". Ainsi sauront-elles offrir "une solidarité généreuse qui commence dans le voisinage immédiat pour s'ouvrir au monde sans frontière".

The gift of grace, faith, prayer and the power of the sacraments are requirements for Christian living, but to them must be added charity, and "love of neighbour." This love is "reconciliation." It is also "will for unity and for fraternity." Such love includes respect and welcome for the poor, and "a search for what is useful for our neighbour," not only in material terms, but in missionary activity.

Community spirit in this country is "undergoing a profound transition." Urban life, the economic crises, and a spiritual crisis–a crisis of values–are affecting community life. But we can "look to the future with serenity" if we "stand firm" in faith, and allow the spirit of Christ to form "responses to the new challenges." We should "show solidarity with one another" and "accept being a leaven in the Church and in society."

Faith will help communities to take up these new challenges. Sharing, justice, charity need to be "rooted in spiritual energy." We must "revive the faith" and it will include all the commitments of charity–respect for persons, respect for human rights, and respect for life, opposition to violence, concern for less fortunate people, the establishment of social measures for greater equality and justice, a missionary zeal, and a will to simplicity and sharing.

Communities should be "open to the spirit of Christ." Then they will be able "to provide a generous sharing that begins in the immediate neighbourhood and that opens up, without boundaries, to the world."

Il dono di grazia, fede, preghiera, e il vigore dei sacramenti sono delle condizioni per il vivere cristiano, ma bisogna aggiungervi la carità e "l'amore per il prossimo." Questo amore è "riconciliazione." È anche "desidero di unità e fratellanza." Significa rispetto e ospitalità verso i poveri, e "ricerca di ciò che è utile per il nostro prossimo," non solo provvedendo ai bisogni materiali ma anche svolgendo attività missionaria.

Lo spirito di comunità in questo paese sta "subendo una profonda trasformazione." La vita cittadina, le crisi economiche e una crisi spirituale – una crisi di valori – colpiscono la vita di comunità. Ma possiamo "guardare con serenità al futuro" se "ci manteniamo saldi" nella fede e lasciamo che lo spirito di Cristo dia "delle risposte ai nuovi interrogativi." Dobbiamo "mostrare reciproca solidarietà" e "accettare di essere il lievito della Chiesa e della società."

La fede aiuterà le comunità ad affrontare queste nuove prove. La comunione con gli altri, la giustizia, la carità hanno bisogno di essere "radicate nell'energia spirituale." Dobbiamo "far rivivere la fede," e ciò significherà anche affrontare tutti gli impegni di carità – il rispetto per le persone, per i diritti umani e per la vita umana, il rifiuto della violenza, la sollecitudine verso i meno fortunati, e la costituzione di nuove misure sociali che conducano a maggiore uguaglianza e giustizia, zelo missionario, apprezzamento delle cose semplici e comunione con gli altri.

Le comunità dovrebbero essere "aperte allo spirito di Cristo." Allora esse saranno in grado di "fornire un generoso contributo che, partendo dal loro immediato vicinato, si apre, senza confini, al mondo intero."

Chrześcijańskie życie stawia przed nami pewne wymagania, lecz do tych wymagań, jak dar łaski, wiara, modlitwa, moc sakramentu, należy dodać miłosierdzie oraz "umiłowanie bliźniego". Jest to „pojednanie", „wola jedności i braterstwa", respekt i przyjazny stosunek do biednych, „niesienie pomocy bliźniemu" nie tylko materialnej, lecz również duchowej.

W życiu duchowym społeczności w tym kraju zachodzą gruntowne przemiany. Wielkomiejskie życie, kryzysy ekonomiczne oraz kryzysy duchowe—kryzysy wartości— mają duży wpływ na życie społeczności. Lecz będziemy mogli „patrzeć w przyszłość ze spokojem", jeżeli „nie odstąpimy" wiary i poddamy się woli Chrystusa, z którego pomocą, znajdziemy siły do walki z „nowymi problemami, które niesie życie". Powinniśmy demonstrować „wzajemną solidarność" oraz zaakceptować fakt bycia zaczynem w życiu Kościoła i społeczności".

Wiara dopomoże w podjęciu tych nowych obowiązków. Hojność, sprawiedliwość, miłosierdzie muszą być „zakorzenione w duchowej energii". Musimy „ożywić wiarę", która włączy w siebie wszystkie zobowiazania miłosierdzia—respekt dla ludzi, respekt dla praw człowieka oraz respekt dla życia, walkę z przemocą, troskę o ludzi w potrzebie, socjalną ustawę o większą równość i sprawiedliwość, misjonarską gorliwość, jak również wolę ułatwiania oraz uczestniczenia.

Społeczności muszą być zawsze „gotowe do przyjęcia Chrystusa". Tylko wtedy będą mogły „wnieść hojny wkład w społeczność, najpierw tą najbliższą, a następnie w zasięgu światowym, gdyż dla spraw duchowych nie ma granic".

... L'amour est recherche
    de ce qui est utile au prochain ...

... Love is a search for what is useful
    for our neighbour ...

... Amore è ricerca di ciò
    che è bene per il nostro prossimo ...

... Miłość jest pomocą
    niesioną bliźniemu ...

"Ce que nous avons reçu comme un don, il nous faut l'offrir" comme un don. Il faut partager avec les autres le grand don de la communion avec Dieu. Le Pape Jean-Paul II affirme vouloir "partager d'une façon particulière" les richesses du mystère de la liturgie.

La mission de l'Église consiste, entre autres, à proclamer le mystère de Dieu et à "conduire l'humanité entière" à la foi. "Par le baptême et la confirmation, chacun est appelé à participer à la mission salvatrice de l'Église."

L'évangélisation et le zèle missionnaire sont "le patrimoine sacré du Canada". L'Église du Canada a "pris une grande part à l'effort missionnaire de l'Église universelle à travers le monde".

Le zèle missionnaire

Missionary Activity

L'attività missionaria

Działalność Misjonarska

"What we have received as a gift, however, we must give as a gift. The great gift of communion with God must be shared with others." Pope John Paul II says that he wants "to share in a special way" the riches of the mystery of the liturgy.

This sharing of the mystery and leading "all humanity" to faith is part of the mission of the Church, and through "Baptism and Confirmation everyone is called to share in the saving mission of the Church."

Evangelization and missionary activity are "the sacred heritage of Canada" because of its history of such activity both at home and abroad. The Church of Canada has "played a considerable role in the missionary effort of the Universal Church throughout the world."

"Ma ciò che abbiamo ricevuto in dono, dobbiamo darlo in dono. Il grande dono della comunione con Dio deve essere diviso con gli altri." Papa Giovanni Paolo II dice di volere "dividere, in maniera speciale," le ricchezze del mistero liturgico.

Rendere partecipi del mistero e guidare "tutta l'umanità" verso la fede è parte della missione della Chiesa, e attraverso "il Battesimo e la Cresima ciascuno è chiamato a essere partecipe della missione salvatrice della Chiesa."

L'evangelizzazione e l'attività missionaria sono "la sacra eredità del Canada," derivatagli dalla storia stessa di questa sua attività, svolta nel Paese e fuori di esso. La Chiesa canadese "ha svolto una parte di rilievo nello

,,To, co otrzymaliśmy w darze, musimy oddać jako dar. Wielki dar łączności duchowej z Bogiem musimy dzielić z innymi". Papież Jan Paweł II mowi, iż pragnie ,,w szczególny sposób" podzielić się bogactwem tajemnicy liturgicznej.

Powierzenie tajemnicy oraz prowadzenie ,,całej ludzkości" do wiary, jest częścią misji Kościoła, a poprzez chrzest oraz bierzmowanie, każdy jest zaproszony do udziału w zbawiennej misji Kościoła".

Dzięki historii działalności misjonarskiej, oraz nawracaniu w kraju i za granicą, nawracanie oraz działalność misjonarska stały się ,,świętym dziedzictwem Kanady". Kościół Kanadyjski

Chacun a un rôle à jouer dans la mission de l'Église. Non seulement les religieux qui y consacrent leur vie, mais encore les laïcs "qui sont appelés à témoigner du Christ dans la sphère de [leurs] foyers, [leur] voisinage, [leurs] villages et [leurs] villes".

Les laïcs peuvent encore "renouveler l'ordre temporel" en infusant "l'esprit chrétien dans la mentalité et le mode de vie, dans les lois et les structures [de la] communauté" dans laquelle ils vivent.

Nombreuses sont les manières de considérer cette tâche et de la mener à bien, et "il y a tant à faire".

En parlant au monde d'une façon concrète, nous pouvons "manifester la vérité et la justice" dans notre propre vie, et proclamer notre respect de la vie, notre conscience sociale et notre rejet du matérialisme et des excès de la consommation.

"L'excellente valeur de la vocation missionnaire" doit continuer à s'exercer par le biais du témoignage personnel. Et il faut une cohérence "entre [la] conduite et [la] foi".

Car le fondement et le succès de tout apostolat et de tout ministère reposent sur une vie d'"union vivante avec le Christ […] [entretenue et nourrie] par la prière".

L'Église du Canada sera elle-même "dans la mesure où elle sera chez elle comme à l'étranger, une Église évangélisatrice". Nous devons apporter au monde "les dons de la communion et de l'amour. Nous devons forger des liens de justice et de paix."

Everyone has a role to play in this mission of the Church. Not only religious who have dedicated their lives, but lay people too, are "called to bear witness to Christ within the context of your homes, neighbourhoods, towns and cities."

Laity can also "renew the temporal order" by infusing the "Christian spirit into the mentality and behaviour, the laws and structures of the community" in which they live.

There are many ways to approach and carry on this work, and "There is so much to be done."

By speaking to the world in a practical way, we can "manifest truth and justice" in our own lives and proclaim respect for life, social concern, and rejection of materialism and consumerism.

The "excelling value of the missionary vocation" must continue to be exercised through personal witness. And consistency "between your conduct and your faith" is necessary.

But the foundation and fruitfulness of every apostolate and ministry depend on a life of "intimate union with Christ … maintained and nourished by prayer."

The Church of Canada will be herself "to the extent that she is. at home and abroad, an evangelizing Church." We must bring to the world "the gifts of Communion and love. We must forge the bonds of justice and peace."

sforzo missionario della chiesa universale nel mondo."

E ciascuno ha una parte in tale missione della chiesa. Non solo i religiosi che hanno consacrato le loro vite, ma anche i laici "sono chiamati a portare testimonianza di Cristo nelle loro case, nel loro vicinato e nelle loro città."

I laici possono anche "rinnovare l'ordine temporale" infondendo "lo spirito cristiano nella mentalità e nel comportamento, nelle leggi e nelle strutture della comunità" in cui vivono.

Esistono molti modi per affrontare e continuare questo compito, "e c'è ancora tanto da fare."

Parlando al mondo in maniera pratica, possiamo "manifestare la verità e la giustizia" nelle nostre vite, proclamare il rispetto per la vita, il nostro interesse sociale e il rifiuto del materialismo e del consumismo.

"L'altissimo valore della vocazione missionaria" deve continuare ad essere esercitato attraverso la testimonianza personale. Ed è necessario che "la vostra condotta sia coerente con la vostra fede."

Ma il fondamento e la fecondità di ciascun apostolato e sacerdozio dipendono da una vita di "intima unione con Cristo,… mantenuta e nutrita dalla preghiera."

La stessa Chiesa canadese sarà, "nella misure in cui già lo è, nel Paese e fuori, una Chiesa di evangelizzazione. Dobbiamo portare al mondo "i doni della comunione e dell'amore. Dobbiamo foggiare i vincoli della giustizia e della pace."

„grał istotną rolę w misjonarskich wysiłkach Kościoła Powszechnego na całym świecie".

Każdy ma swoją rolę w tej misji Kościoła. Nie tylko duchowne, lecz i osoby cywilne, „wzywane są do głoszenia wiary w Chrystusa w domach, w pobliskich okolicach, osiedlach i miastach".

Laicy również mogą „odnowić świecki ład" poprzez wszczepienie „chrześcijańskiego ducha w swoją świadomość oraz zachowanie, poprzez zasady i strukturę społeczności", w której żyją.

Jest wiele sposobów podejścia do tego zadania oraz jego kontynuowania, a „Tak wiele jest do zrobienia".

Zwracając się do świata w sposób praktyczny, możemy „manifestować prawdę i sprawiedliwość" w naszym własnym życiu, proklamować respekt dla życia, troskę o socjalny byt, odrzucenie materializmu oraz konsumpcyjnosci.

Życie osobiste musi podkreślać „wielką wartość misjonarskiego powołania". Konieczną jest harmonia „między zachowaniem i wiarą Waszą".

Trwałość oraz płodność każdego apostolatu i kapłaństwa, zależy od „bliskiej jedności z Chrystusem … podtrzymywanej i pielęgnowanej przez modlitwę".

Kościół Kanadyjski, będzie „w pełnej mierze, zarówno w domu, jak i za granicą, Kościołem głoszącym Ewangelię". Musimy przekazać światu „dary łączności duchowej i miłości. Musimy rozkuć kajdany sprawiedliwości i pokoju".

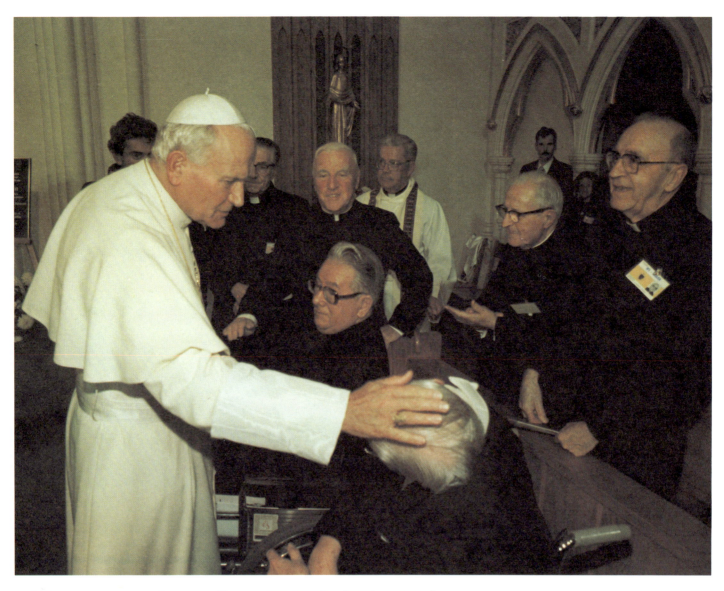

... Je viens célébrer
avec vous notre foi
en Jésus-Christ ...

... I come to celebrate
with you our Faith
in Jesus Christ ...

... Vengo a celebrare
con voi la nostra fede
in Gesù Cristo ...

... Przychodzę sławić
z Wami naszą Wiarę
w Jezusa Chrystusa ...

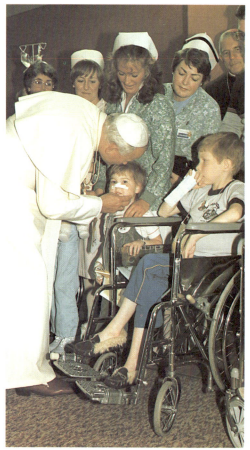

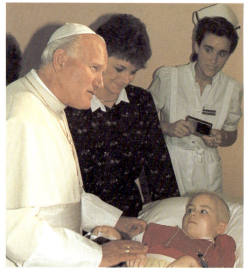

... La vie liturgique
de l'Église appartient
à tous les fidèles ...

... the liturgical life
of the Church belongs
to all the faithful ...

... La vita liturgica
della Chiesa appartiene
a tutti i fedeli ...

... Życie liturgiczne
Kościoła, należy
do wszystkich wiernych ...

L'homme et la technologie

Technology and the Human Person

La technologia e l'uomo

Postep Techniczny i Człowiek

"J'en appelle à vous tous de considérer la technologie dans le contexte du message de la Croix et de faire votre part afin que ce pouvoir technologique serve la cause de l'espoir." Le Pape Jean-Paul II nous rappelle que la technologie peut faire changer le monde, mais n'apporte pas de véritable réponse au mystère de notre destinée.

L'humanité est "largement submergée dans les promesses et les problèmes de la technologie et tentée d'embrasser une mentalité technologique". La technologie a "contribué au bien-être de l'humanité; elle a tant fait pour améliorer la condition humaine, servir l'humanité et faciliter son labeur".

"Pourtant, à certains moments, la technologie ne sait plus vraiment […] [si elle est] pour l'humanité ou contre elle." Cette même technologie qui peut aider les pauvres "contribue parfois elle-même à la pauvreté, réduit les possibilités de travailler et étouffe le potentiel de la créativité humaine". Elle cesse alors d'être l'alliée de l'homme.

Une technologie en expansion rapide peut être bénéfique, mais elle produit également "une mentalité technologique hostile aux valeurs évangéliques". "La tentation existe de poursuivre le développement technologique en tant que valeur propre" au lieu de "le considérer comme une richesse à mettre au service de la famille humaine". On peut être tenté de lier la technologie à la "logique du profit […] sans égard pour les droits des travailleurs ou les besoins des pauvres et des démunis". Enfin, cette technologie peut être

"View technology within the context of the message of the Cross and … do your part so that the power of technology will serve the cause of hope." Pope John Paul II reminds us that technology "makes it possible to change the world but brings no real answer to the mystery of our destiny."

Humanity is "immersed to a great extent in the promises and problems of technology and tempted to embrace a technological mentality." That technology has "contributed so much to the well-being of humanity; it has done so much to uplift the human condition, to serve humanity, and to facilitate and perfect its work."

But there are times when "technology cannot decide … whether it is for humanity or against it." The same technology that can help the poor "sometimes even contributes to poverty, limits the opportunities for work and removes the possibility of human creativity." Then it ceases to be an ally of humanity.

A rapidly expanding technology can be beneficial but has also "ushered in a technological mentality which challenges Gospel values." There is a

"Guardate alla tecnologia entro il contesto del messaggio della Croce e … contribuite a che il potere tecnologico serve la causalavoro speranza." Papa Giovanni Paolo II ci ricorda che la tecnologia "può cambiare il mondo, ma non dà nessuna vera risposta al mistero del nostro destino."

L'umanità è "immersa in larga misura nelle promesse e nei problemi tecnologici, ed è tentata di abbracciare una mentalità tecnologica. Questa tecnologia ha "tanto contribuito al benessere dell'umanità; ha fatto molto per migliorare le condizioni umane, per servire l'umanità e per facilitarne e perfezionarne il lavoro."

Me ci sono volte in cui "la tecnologia non sa decidere se essere per l'umanità o contro di essa." Quella stessa tecnologia che può aiutare i poveri "qualche volta contribuisce perfino a creare povertà, limita le opportunità di lavoro e distrugge le possibilità della creatività dell'uomo." Allora essa cessa di essere un'alleata dell'umanità.

Una tecnologia in rapida espansione può portare benefici, ma ha anche "portato con sè una mentalità tecnologicà che sfida i valori evangelici." C'è la tentazione di perseguire il processo tecnologico fine a sè stesso," invece di "vederlo come una risorsa da mettere al servizio dell'umana famiglia." La

„Wykonujcie swoją pracę tak, aby postęp techniczny służył ludzkości i wzbudzał nadzieję, patrzcie na niego z punktu widzenia posłannictwa Krzyża …" Papież Jan Paweł II przypomina, że postęp techniczny „może zmienić świat, lecz nie daje odpowiedzi na pytanie o tajemnicy naszego przeznaczenia".

Ludzkość jest „całkowicie uzależniona od obietnic i problemów techniki, jest skłonna do przyjęcia mentalności technicznej". Technika ma wielki wkład w dobro ludzkości, zrobiła tak wiele, aby poprawić warunki ludzkiego bytu, aby służyć ludzkości, aby ułatwić i udoskonalić warunki pracy".

Lecz są momenty, kiedy „technika nie może zadecydować … co jest dla, a co przeciw ludzkości". Ta sama technika, która może pomóc biednym, „czasami przyczynia się do zubożenia, ogranicza szanse znalezienia pracy, pozbawia ludzi ich możliwości twórczych". W ten sposób przestaje być sprzymierzeńcem ludzkości.

Gwałtownie rozwijająca się technika przynosi korzyści, lecz jednocześnie „wprowadza mentalność techniczną, która kwestionuje wartosci święte". Są próby wykorzystania „postępu technicznego dla własnych jego korzyści", zamiast „widzieć w

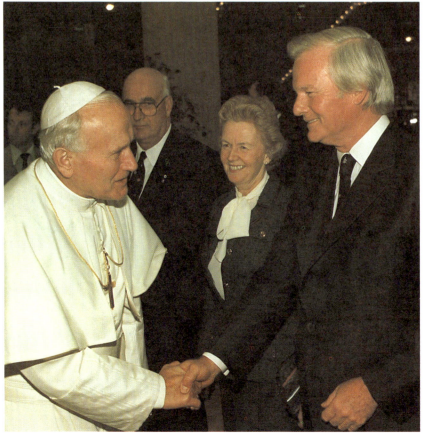

... La valeur de la vie
réside dans ce que vous êtes ...

... The value of life
lies in who you are ...

... Il valore della vita
risiede in chi si è ...

... Wartość życia jest
w tym, kim jesteś ...

rattachée à "la poursuite [...] du pouvoir" au lieu d'être "un instrument de la liberté".

"Tout développement technologique doit être examiné à la lumière des exigences objectives de l'ordre moral et à la lumière du message évangélique."

Le Christ continue d'adresser à son Père sa supplique pour "l'édification d'une terre nouvelle, une terre qui soit plus humaine parce que touchée par l'amour d'une mère – Sa Mère et la nôtre". La prière et l'amour de sa mère sont offerts à tous ceux et celles qui ressentent les souffrances et les défis de ce monde technologique, surtout "aux chômeurs et à tous ceux d'entre vous qui sont victimes de la crise économique et qui en subissent les conséquences sociales". Ils apportent "à toute l'humanité l'assurance de l'amour maternel et de l'attention personnelle, pour chaque individu, chaque personne humaine".

De nombreuses personnes composent la société technologique : "travailleurs de l'industrie; ceux qui sont engagés dans les activités de la finance, du commerce, de l'éducation, de l'édition, de l'informatique, de la recherche médicale, des arts; animateurs de communautés; ceux et celles qui emploient, directement ou indirectement, des millions de personnes".

Et quiconque le peut doit apporter sa contribution pour que la technologie "serve véritablement chaque homme, chaque femme et chaque enfant de ce pays".

"À l'heure de son triomphe ultime", la technologie peut nous conduire à proclamer la "suprématie" de la "sagesse divine qui rend possible la technologie mais qui, du haut de la Croix du Christ, nous en révèle les limites mêmes".

temptation to pursue "technological development for its own sake" instead of "seeing it as a resource to be placed at the service of the human family." Technology can be tied to the "logic of profit … without due regard for the rights of workers or the needs of the poor and helpless." It can become part of the "pursuit of power" instead of an "instrument for freedom."

"All such developments need to be examined in terms of the objective demands of the moral order and in the light of the Gospel message."

Christ continues to plead with the Father for "the building of a new earth, one that is more human because it is embraced by the love of a Mother – his Mother and ours." His prayer and the love of his Mother are offered for all those who experience the pain and challenges of this world of technology, especially the "unemployed and all of you who are caught in the coils of an economic crisis and suffer its social effects." They offer "all humanity the reassurance of loving care and personal concern for each individual, each human person."

Many people make up technological society – "workers in industry, finance, commerce, education, publishing, information, medical research, the arts … leaders in communities … direct and indirect employers of millions of people."

And everyone who can should make a contribution to ensure that technology "will truly serve man, woman, and child throughout this land."

In its "final and greatest triumph" technology may lead us to proclaim the "magnitude" of the Divine wisdom which makes technology possible, but which from the Cross of Christ "reveals the very limitations of this technology."

tecnologia può essere asservita "alla logica del profitto, … senza la giusta considerazione per i diritti dei lavoratori o i bisogni dei poveri e degli indifesi." E può diventare parte della corsa al potere, invece di uno strumento di libertà."

Tutti questi sviluppi devono essere esaminati nei termini delle esigenze oggettive dell'ordine morale e alla luce del messaggio evangelico."

Cristo continua a intercedere presso il Padre per "l'edificazione di un mondo nuovo, più umano perché circondato dall'amore di una Madre – Madre Sua e nostra." La preghiera di Cristo e l'amore della Madre Sua sono offerti per tutti coloro che sopportano le dure prove e le sofferenze di questo mondo tecnologico, specialmente "i disoccupati e tutti coloro fra voi che sono presi nella morsa della crisi economica e ne soffrono le conseguenze sociali." Le Sue preghiere offrono "a tutta l'umanità la sicurezza di amorevole protezione e interessamento personale per ogni singolo individuo, per ogni essere umano."

Molte persone costituiscono una società tecnologica: "coloro che lavorano nelle industrie, nelle finanze, nel commercio, nel sistema scolastico, nell'editoria, nell'informazione, nella ricerca medica, nelle arti … i capi delle comunità, … i datori di lavoro diretti o indiretti di milioni di persone."

E tutti coloro che ne sono in grado dovrebbero contribuire a che la tecnologia "serva veramente gli uomini, le donne e i bambini in ogni parte di questo Paese."

Nel suo "più alto e finale trionfo" la tecnologia può condurci a proclamare "la grandezza" della sapienza divina che rende possibile la tecnologia, ma che dalla voce di Cristo, "ne rivela gli stessi limiti."

nim zasoby, które mogłyby być użyte dla służenia rodzinie ludzkiej". Technika „ma na uwadze jedynie korzyść, bez uwzględnienia praw robotników lub potrzeb biednych i bezradnych". W ten sposób rozwój techniki staje się „pogonią za władzą", zamiast być „kluczem do wolności".

Tego rodzaju postęp musi być przeegzaminowany z punktu widzenia obiektywnych potrzeb moralnych oraz w świetle nauki ewangelickiej".

Chrystus bezustannie wstawia się do Ojca swego „za odnowicieli świata, który stanie się bardziej ludzki, otoczony opieką i miłością Matki – Matki Jego i naszej". Modlitwa Chrystusa oraz miłość Matki Jego, zawsze są po stronie cierpiących z powodu świata postępu technicznego, a zwłaszcza „bezrobotni i wy wszyscy, którzyście wpadli w sidła kryzysów ekonomicznych i cierpicie z powodu tych kryzysów". Chrystus i Matka Jego „zapewniają ludzkość o swojej serdecznej opiece i osobistej trosce o każdego człowieka, każdą istotę ludzką".

Na techniczne społeczeństwo składa się wiele osób — „robotnicy w przemyśle, pracownicy w handlu, szkolnictwie, wydawnictwie, informacji, lekarze, ludzie sztuki … pracownicy społeczni, pośredni i bezpośredni pracodawcy milionów ludzi".

Każdy, kto może, powinien wnieść swój wkład, aby zapewnić, że technika „w Kanadzie będzie szczerze służyła człowiekowi — mężczyznom, kobietom i dzieciom".

W jej „ostatecznym i wspaniałym triumfie" technika może doprowadzić nas do ogłoszenia „wielkości" mądrości Boskiej, dzięki której postęp techniczny jest możliwy, lecz która zarazem, z punktu widzenia Krzyża Chrystusowego, „odsłania jej słabe strony".

... Le travail d'évangélisation porte fruit lorsque les Chrétiens des différentes communions, bien que non encore pleinement unis, collaborent comme frères et sœurs en Jésus-Christ ...

... The work of evangelization bears fruit when Christians of different communions, though not yet fully one, collaborate as brothers and sisters in Christ ...

... L'evangelizzazione porta frutti quando i fedeli di diverse confessioni, sebbene non completamente uniti, collaborano come fratelli e sorelle in Cristo ...

... Wysiłki ewangelickie wydają płody wtedy tylko, gdy chrześcijanie różnych wspólnot, współpracują jako bracia i siostry w Chrystusie ...

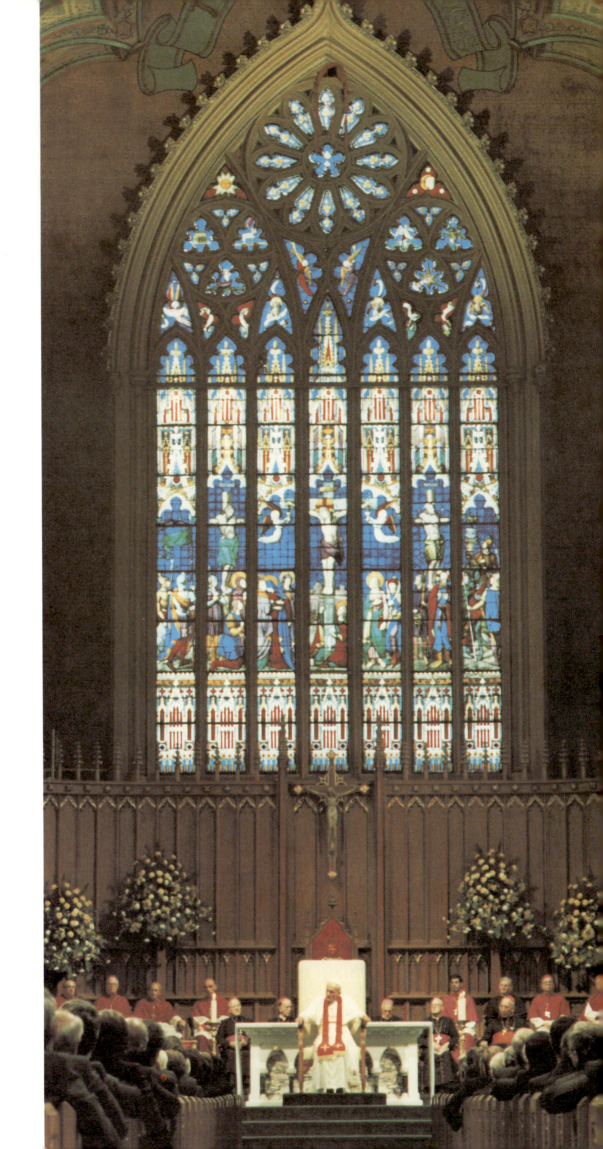

... Seule la Parole
de Dieu donne la clé
de notre existence,
éclaire nos chemins ...

... Only the word
of God holds the key
to our existence and
enlightens our paths ...

... Solo la parola
di Dio regge
le chiavi della nostra
esistenza ed illumina
il nosto cammino ...

... Tylko słowo Boże
zawiera klucz
do naszego życia
i oświetla
ścieżki nasze ...

... Laissons-nous
saisir par
l'Esprit
du Christ ...

... Let us
allow ourselves
to be seized by
the Spirit
of Christ ...

... Lasciamo che
lo Spirito di Cristo
di impadronisca
di noi ...

... Pozwólmy
Duchowi
Chrystusowemu
zawładnąć sobą ...

98

... Le monde a besoin de témoins
de la gratuité de l'amour de Dieu ...

... The world needs witnesses
to the free gift of the love of God ...

... Il mondo ha bisogno di testimoni
del dono d'amore Divino ...

... Świat potrzebuje dowodów
darmowego daru Bożej Miłości ...

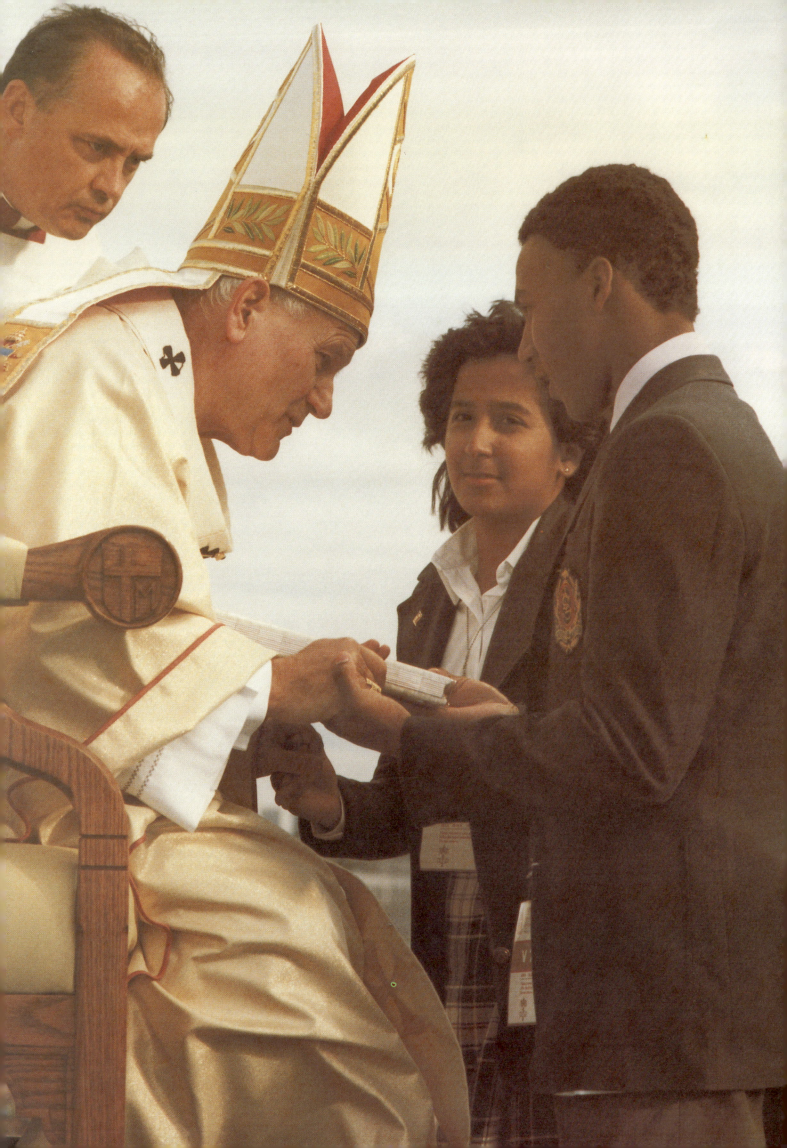

Foi et multiculturalisme

Faith and Multiculturalism

Fede e Multiculturalismo

Wiara i Wielokulturowość

"L'Évangile est devenu – et il ne cesse de l'être – une source de culture spirituelle pour les hommes et les femmes de toutes les nations, de toutes les langues et de toutes les races." Le Pape Jean-Paul II affirme encore que l'Évangile est également "la base du caractère individuel et de l'identité culturelle de nombreux peuples et nations du monde entier".

"C'est dans cette perspective de foi que nous comprenons à quel point la Parole de Dieu […] contribue à l'édification et à la préservation des cultures." Le message de l'Évangile est nécessaire pour "harmoniser les cultures en une unité pluraliste".

Même dans l'ordre civil, "l'Évangile est au service de l'harmonie", car séparer la culture de son lien intime avec le commandement d'amour "rendrait impossible cette imbrication multiculturelle qui est la caractéristique du Canada".

"Le pluralisme des traditions, le pluralisme des cultures, le pluralisme des histoires et le pluralisme des identités nationales – tous sont compatibles avec l'unité de la société." Mais nous avons surtout besoin de "l'unité morale" de la société, fondement de tous les "besoins civils".

"The Gospel has become–and always continues to become–the source of spiritual culture for men and women of different nations, tongues and races." Pope John Paul II says that the Gospel is also "the basis of the individual and cultural identity of many peoples and nations throughout the world."

In the perspective of faith we perceive how much the Word of God … contributes to the building and preservation of cultures. And the Gospel message is needed for success in "harmonizing cultures in a pluralistic society."

Even in the civil order, the "gospel is at the service of harmony" since to detach culture from its link to love "would be to make impossible the cultural interplay which is characteristic of Canada."

"Pluralism of traditions, pluralism of cultures, pluralism of histories, pluralism of national identities–all of these are compatible with the unity of society." But we need especially the "moral unity" of society, the foundation of the civil.

"Il Vangelo è diventato – e continua ancora a diventare la sorgente di cultura spirituale per uomini e donne di varie nazioni, linque e razze." Papa Giovanni Paolo II dice che il Vangelo è anche "la base dell'identità individuale e culturale di molti popoli nel mondo."

Nella prospettiva della fede noi ci rendiamo conto quanto la Parola di Dio contribuisce alla edificazione e alla conservazione delle culture. E il messaggio evangelico è necessario perché si possano " armonizzare le culture in una società pluralistica."

Anche nell'ordine civile il "Vangelo è al servizio dell'armonia," poichè staccare la cultura dal suo vincolo con l'amore significherebbe rendere impossibile l'interscambio culturale che è caratteristico del Canada."

"Pluralismo di tradizioni, pluralismo di culture, pluralismo di storie, pluralismo di identità nazionali – tutto ciò è compatibile con l'unità sociale." Ma abbiamo bisogno soprattutto dell' "unità morale" della società fondamento della civiltà.

„Ewangelia stała się – i w dalszym ciągu jest – źródłem kultury duchowej dla mężczyzn i kobiet różnych narodowości, języków i ras". Papież Jan Paweł II również mówi, że Ewangelia jest także „podstawą tożsamości indywidualnej i kulturowej wielu nacji i narodowości na całym świecie".

Z perspektywy wiary uświadamiamy sobie, jak wiele Słowo Boże … daje wkładu w tworzenie i zachowanie kultur. Nauki Ewangelii konieczne są, aby z powodzeniem osiągnąć cel „zharmonizowania kultur w wielonarodowościowym społeczeństwie".

Nawet w ładzie państwowym „ewangelia służy harmonii", jako że, gdyby oddzielić kulturę od jej więzi z miłością, „wzajemne oddziaływanie kultur, co jest cechą charakterystyczną Kanady, stałoby się niemożliwym".

„Pluralizm tradycji, pluralizm kultur, pluralizm historii, pluralizm narodowych tożsamości – wszystko to daje się pogodzić z jednością społeczeństwa". W szczególności jednak potrzebna jest „jedność moralna" społeczeństwa, podstawy państwa.

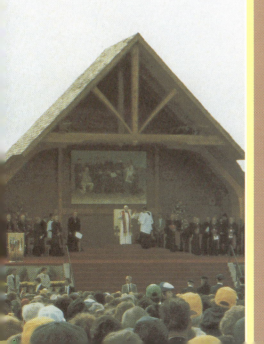

"Un riche patrimoine de peuples, de nations et de cultures devient le bien commun de toute la société."

Le christianisme a toujours demandé aux personnes "de se sentir responsables du bien commun de la société", même lorsque cette société a manifestement des caractéristiques pluralistes. "Le fondement de cet enseignement se trouve dans le commandement d'amour mutuel."

L'amour mutuel signifie "les rapports entre êtres humains, bâtis sur le respect de la dignité individuelle de l'autre et sur le souci authentique de son véritable bien-être".

Il revêt une importance particulière pour la famille et s'étend également à des communautés et des sociétés nombreuses et diverses. Cet amour est donc "social" et "constitue la condition essentielle" à cette "civilisation d'amour que proclame l'Église".

Le Canada se caractérise par un climat de respect de la diversité culturelle. Par cette interaction multiculturelle, il offre au monde "une vision créatrice de la société".

.

Cette ouverture d'esprit et cet "accueil généreux" des Canadiens à l'endroit des immigrants, des réfugiés et des minorités ethniques est caractéristique. "La plus grande richesse de ton caractère multiculturel est cette possibilité qui t'est donnée d'aller vers autrui pour lui apporter ton aide."

En réunissant ces talents multiples dans l'amour, "une société multiculturelle peut alors faire rejaillir sur autrui toutes ces bénédictions dont elle a été abondamment gratifiée".

"A varied inheritance of peoples, nations and cultures becomes the common good of the whole of society."

Christianity has always asked people to "have a sense of responsibility for the common good of society" even when the society has clearly pluralistic characteristics. This teaching is based on "the commandment of mutual love."

Mutual love means the "relationship between human beings based on respect for the personal dignity of the other person and on real care for his or her true good."

It has special importance in the family, but extends to many different circles, communities, societies. This love is thus "social" and "constitutes the essential condition" for the "civilization of love" proclaimed by the church.

Canada is characterized by "an atmosphere of respect for cultural diversity". Multicultural interaction offers the world "a creative vision of society".

The openness and "generous reception" of Canadians to immigrants and refugees of ethnic minorities are characteristic. The "greatest richness of your multicultural character is to be able to reach out and help others."

By uniting the various talents through love, a multicultural society "is able to place at the disposal of others all those blessings which it has so bountifully received."

"Una eredità composita di popoli, nazioni e culture diventa una ricchezze comune di tutta la società."

Il Cristianesimo ha sempre chiesto agli uomini di "nutrire un senso di responsabilità per il bene comune della società," anche quando la società presenta delle chiare caratteristiche di pluralismo. Tale insegnamento è basato sul "comandamento dell'amore reciproco."

L'amore reciproco è "il rapporto fra esseri umani basato sul rispetto della dignità personale del prossimo e sul reale interesse al suo bene."

Esso è importante in special modo nelle famiglie, ma si estende a differenti circoli, comunità, società. Tale amore è quindi "sociale" e "costituisce la condizione essenziale per la "civiltà dell'amore" proclamata dalla Chiesa.

Il Canada è caratterizzato da "un' atmosfera di rispetto per le diversità culturali." Le interazioni multiculturali offrono al mondo "una visione creativa della società."

L'apertura e la "generosa accoglienza" dei Canadesi nei confronti degli immigrati, dei rifugiati e delle minoranze etniche sono caratteristiche. La "maggior ricchezza del vostro carattere multiculturalista è la capacità di tendere una mano ed aiutare gli altri."

Unificando le varie potenzialità attraverso l'amore, una società multiculturalista "è in grado di mettere a disposizione di altri tutti i doni del cielo che ha ricevuto in così grande abbondanza."

„Różne narodowe dziedzictwa, narodowości i kultury, stają się ogólnym dobrem całego społeczeństwa".

Chrześcijaństwo zawsze wymagało od ludzi „poczucia odpowiedzialności za dobro ogólne społeczeństwa", nawet jeżeli społeczeństwo miało wyraźnie charakter pluralistyczny. Ta nauka oparta jest na „przykazaniu o wzajemnej miłości".

Wzajemna miłość, oznacza „wzajemny stosunek między ludźmi, oparty na respektowaniu osobistej godności innych osób i prawdziwej trosce o jego, lub jej dobro".

Ważne to jest w rodzine, lecz rozprzestrzenia się również na wiele rożnych kręgów, społeczności i społeczeństw. A więc miłość ta, jest „społeczna" i „stanowi istotny warunek" dla „cywilizacji miłości" proklamowanej przez Kościół.

Kanadę znamionuje „atmosfera szacunku dla kulturowej różnorodności". Świat obserwuje tworzenie się, na skutek wzajemnego oddziaływania wielu kultur, nowego typu społeczeństwa.

Szczerość i „hojność przyjęcia" emigrantów, uciekinierów i mniejszości etnicznych przez Kanadyjczyków są bardzo znamienne. „Największym skarbem Waszego wielokulturowego charakteru, jest chęć pomocy innym".

Jednocząc różne talenty poprzez miłość, wielokulturowe społeczeństwo jest w stanie zaoferować innym wszystkie te błogosławieństwa, które tak szczodrze samo otrzymało".

... Faites que votre peuple chrétien
s'abreuve à la Source vive
elle-même ...

... Lead your Christian people
to drink from the Living Water ...

... Conduci il tuo popolo cristiano
a bere l'Acqua della Vita ...

... Prowadź swój chrześcijański
lud do źrodła Wody Życia,
aby z niego pił ...

... J'embrasse tous et chacun
par mon cœur, et je transmets
un baiser de paix comme Pape
et comme frère ...

... I give a heartfelt greeting
and embrace to you in peace
as Pope and brother ...

... In pace vi abbraccio
e vi saluto di cuore
come Papa e fratello ...

... Przekazuję Wam, w pokoju,
najszczersze pozdrowienia
i uściski jako Papież i brat ...

Le Canada et le Tiers-Monde

Canada and the Third World

Il Canada e il Terzo Mondo

Kanada i Trzeci Świat

"Le développement des peuples est une question de la plus haute importance, relevant de la responsabilité sociale et internationale." Le Pape Jean-Paul II nous dit que la fraternité du Christ avec chaque personne est en même temps fraternité avec l'ensemble de la race humaine.

Nous devons penser que chaque fois que nous faisons du bien à "un être humain dans le besoin", nous le faisons au Christ. Mais nous ne pouvons pas nous en tenir à une interprétation "individualiste" de la morale chrétienne, car elle possède "également une dimension sociale. La personne humaine vit en communauté, en société. Elle partage avec cette communauté la faim, la soif, la maladie, la malnutrition, la misère et tous les maux qui en dérivent. L'être humain ressent dans sa propre personne les besoins des autres."

La charité chrétienne, c'est parler "de la dimension universelle de l'injustice et du mal". À l'heure actuelle, c'est surtout parler "de ce que nous avons coutume d'appeler le contraste Nord-Sud". Le Sud devient "de plus en plus pauvre" et le Nord "de plus en plus riche".

"The development of peoples is a question of greatest importance and social and international responsibility." Pope John Paul II says that the brotherhood of Christ with every single person means our brotherhood with the whole human race.

We must consider that each time we do good for "an individual human being in need" we do it for Christ. But we cannot stop at an individualistic interpretation of Christian ethics, since it "also has its social dimension." The human person "lives in a community, in society. And with the community he shares hunger and thirst and sickness and malnutrition and misery and all the deficiencies that result therefrom. In his or her own person the human being is meant to experience the needs of others."

Christian charity is speaking "of the whole universal dimension of injustice and evil." Of

"Lo svluppo dei popoli è una questione della massima importanza e responsabilità sociale e internazionale." Papa Giovanni Paolo II dice che la fratellanza di Cristo con ogni singolo individuo significa la fratellanza nostra con l'intero genere umano.

Dobbiamo tener presente che ogni qual volta facciamo del bene "a un singolo essere umano bisognoso," lo facciamo a Cristo. Ma non possiamo limitarci a un'interpretazione individualista dell'etica cristiana, poiché essa "ha anche una sua dimensione sociale." L'essere umamo "vive in una comunità, in una società. E con la comunità divide fame e sete, malattie, denutrizione, miseria, e tutte le sofferenze che da ciò derivano. L'essere umano deve conoscere sulla propria persona i bisogni altrui."

Carità cristiana è parlare "di tutta la dimensione universale dell'ingiustizia e del male." Di particolare importanza, oggi, è "ciò che abitualmente definiamo come il contrasto nord-sud." Il sud "diventa sempre più povero, e il nord sempre più ricco."

„Rozwój narodów jest problemem o wielkim znaczeniu oraz odpowiedzialnością zarówno socjalną, jak i międzynarodową". Papież Jan Paweł II podkreslił, że braterstwo Chrystusa z każdym człowiekiem, oznacza nasze braterstwo z całą ludzkością.

Musimy pamiętać, że wspomagając „każdą istotę ludzką w potrzebie", robimy to dla Chrystusa. Lecz nie możemy organiczyć się w interpretacji etyki chrześcijańskiej, do jednostek, gdyż „posiada ona swoje socjalne wymiary". Człowiek „żyje w społeczności, w społeczeństwie i z nimi dzieli głód i pragnienie, chorobę i niedożywienie, niedolę i wszystkie braki, jako rezultat tego. Każdy człowiek musi poznać potrzeby innych ludzi.

Miłosierdzie chrześcijańskie ma na uwadze „ogólnoświatowe wymiary zła i niesprawiedliwości". Szczególnie ważnym w dniu dzisiejszym, jest to, „co przyzwyczailiśmy się określać jako kontrast między Północa i Południem". Południe, „staje się biedniejsze, a północ staje sie bogatsza".

Or, ce sont les peuples et les nations pauvres qui vont juger les riches. Ils souffrent "non seulement [du] manque de nourriture, mais également [de] privation de liberté et des autres droits humains", et ils "jugeront ceux qui leur enlèvent ces biens".

La lutte contre l'injustice n'est pas uniquement la lutte contre le dénuement. Nous devons aider à la construction d'un monde où tout homme, sans distinction de race, de religion ou de nationalité, puisse vivre "une vie pleinement humaine" sans servitude à l'égard des hommes ou de la nature. Ce "développement est le nouveau nom de la paix".

La paix est "un impératif de notre temps", ainsi que le "progrès: le progrès de tous les démunis".

La menace de l'injustice "émane des structures rigides" de ces systèmes qui ne s'ouvrent pas pour aller vers l'homme, vers le développement des peuples, vers la justice et la paix. Le solde global de "ce que nous n'avons pas fait pour le plus petit de nos frères, pour les millions de petits, pour les milliards" s'alourdit.

Mais nous faisons de plus en plus pour le Tiers-Monde, et "ce que nous préparons et ferons avec détermination et une énergie toujours accrue–tout cela compte". Cela entre dans "le solde du bien dans l'histoire humaine".

particular importance today is "what we are accustomed to call the North-South contrast." The south is "becoming always poorer, and the north becoming always richer."

And the poor peoples and nations of the world will judge the rich. They are "not only lacking food, but also deprived of freedom and other human rights" and they will "judge those people who take these goods away from them."

The struggle against injustice is not only against destitution. We must help to build a world where every person, regardless of race, religion, or nationality, can live a "fully human life" without servitude to man or to nature. This development is "the new name" for peace.

Peace is "an imperative of our time," and so is "progress: the progress of all the disadvantaged."

The threat of injustice from the "rigid structure" of systems which do not permit themselves to move towards men, towards the development of peoples, towards justice and peace, the global balance of "what we have not done" for millions and billions of the "least of our brethren" is increasing.

But what we are doing for this "third world" is also increasing and what we "will plan and will do with greater energy and determination–all of this really matters." It is all part of the "balance of good in human history."

E i popoli e le nazioni poveri del mondo giudicheranno ranno quelli ricchi. Essi non solo "mancano di cibo, ma sono anche privati della libertà e degli altri diritti umani," e giudicheranno "i popoli che hanno portato via loro questi beni."

La lotta contro l'ingiustizia non è diretta solo a combattere la misera. Dobbiamo impegnarci ad edificare un mondo in cui ogni individuo, indipendentemente da razza, religione, o nazionalità, può vivere una vita umana nel senso più pieno della parola," libera da schiavitù da uomo o natura. Questo sviluppo è il "nuovo nome" della pace.

La pace è l'imperativo del nostro tempo," come pure il "progresso: il progresso dei meno fortunati."

Aumentano le minacce di ingiustizia da parte "della struttura rigida" di quei sistemi che non permettono a se stessi di andare incontro agli uomini, incontro allo sviluppo dei popoli, incontro alla giustizia e alla pace; aumenta il bilancio globale "di ciò che non abbiamo fatto" per milioni e milioni di "nostri fratelli."

Ma stiamo facendo sempre di più per questo "Terzo Mondo;" e ciò che conta è quello che "ci proponiamo di fare e che faremo con sempre maggiore energia e determinazione." Tutto questo è parte del "bilancio del bene nella storia umana."

A biedne narody i narodowości na całym świecie będą osądzać bogate. „Brakuje im nie tylko żywności, lecz także pozbawieni są wolności i innych praw człowieka „i one będą osądzać tych, którzy od nich te dobra odebrali".

Walka z niesprawiedliwością jest walką nie tylko z nędzą. Musimy zbudować świat, w którym wszyscy, niezależnie od rasy, religii czy narodowości, będzie mógł żyć „pełnią ludzkiego życia". Rozwój, jest „nową nazwą" dla pokoju.

Pokój jest „konieczny w naszych czasach", tak samo „postęp, postęp wszystkich ujemnych stron".

Groźba niesprawiedliwości ze strony „sztywnych" systemów, które nie chcą wyciągnąć ręki w kierunku człowieka, w kierunku rozwoju narodów, w kierunku sprawiedliwości i pokoju, zwiększa swiatowe saldo tego, „czego nie zrobiliśmy" dla milionow i bilionow „najmniejszych naszych braci".

Lecz robimy więcej i więcej dla „trzeciego świata i to, co planujemy i co zrobimy z wielkim zapałem i oddaniem, wszystko to ma znaczenie.

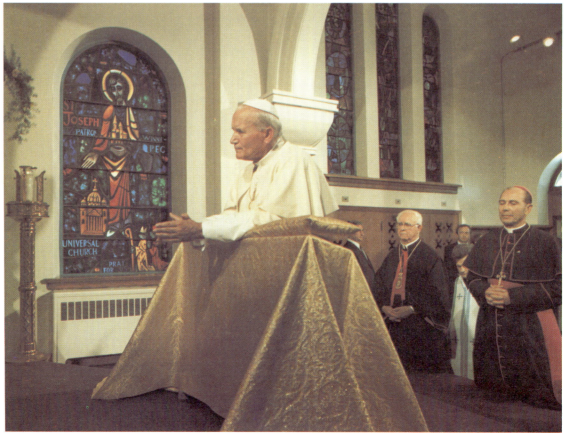

... Enseigner signifie non seulement
communiquer ce que nous savons,
mais également révéler qui nous sommes
en vivant ce que nous croyons ...

... To teach means not only
to impart what we know, but also
to reveal who we are
by living what we believe ...

... L'insegnamento non è solo communicare
quello che sappiamo, ma anche
rivelare chi siamo vivendo
ciò in cui crediamo ...

... Uczyć, znaczy nie tylko przekazać to,
co wiemy, lecz również dać przykład
poprzez życie zgodne z naszą wiarą ...

... L'Eucharistie
est la raison d'être même
du sacerdoce ...

... The Eucharist
is the very reason
for the priesthood ...

... L'Eucharestia
è la ragione prima
per il sacerdozio ...

... Eucharystia
jest prawdziwym powodem
do kapłaństwa ...

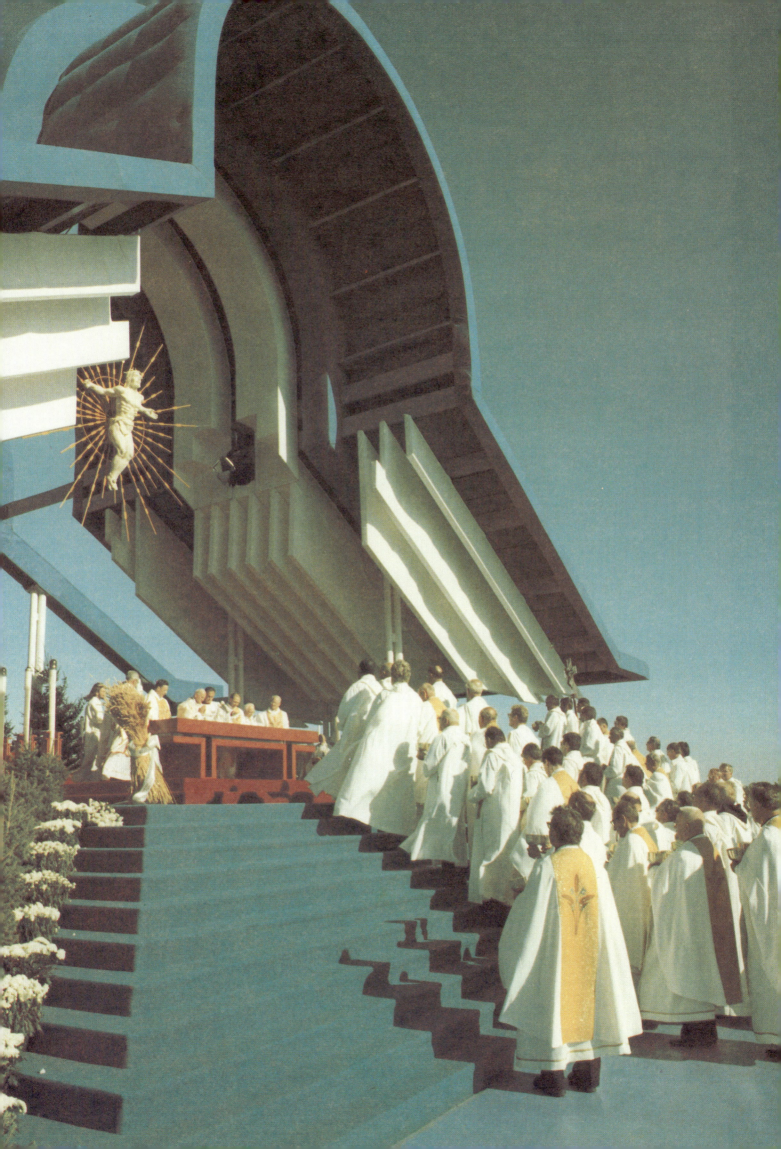

... Que mon pèlerinage
ici soit le symbole
de votre cheminement
dans la foi ...

... May my pilgrimage
here be the symbol
of your journey
in the faith ...

... Possa il mio
pellegrinaggio essere il
simbolo del vostro
viaggio nella fede ...

... Niech moja pielgrzymka
tutaj, będzie symbolem
Waszej wędrówki
w wierze ...

Les autochtones

Native People

Popolazioni nativi

Rdzenna Ludność

"Non seulement le Christianisme est-il très valable pour les peuples indiens, mais le Christ, par les membres de son Corps, est lui-même indien." Et le Pape Jean-Paul II nous redit que l'Évangile "nous appelle à vivre en frères".

Bon nombre d'Amérindiens et d'Inuit d'Amérique du Nord sont chrétiens; ils sont "chrétiens, à part entière, dans l'Église–même s'ils ne le sont pas tout à fait dans la société". Ils ont découvert dans leurs propres cultures "des manières propres" de vivre leur relation avec Dieu et avec le monde.

Loin de détruire les "valeurs et [les] coutumes traditionnelles" de ces autochtones, l'Évangile a "le pouvoir de purifier et d'élever" leur patrimoine culturel. Pendant sa longue histoire, "l'Église elle-même a sans cesse été enrichie" de ces traditions nouvelles.

La rencontre avec l'Évangile ne détruit pas ce qu'il y a de meilleur dans la culture des autochtones, mais elle "féconde comme de l'intérieur les qualités spirituelles et les dons qui sont propres" à ces cultures.

"Not only is Christianity relevant to the native peoples, but Christ, in the members of his Body, is Indian." Pope John Paul II reminds us that the Gospel "calls us to live as his brothers and sisters."

Many Amerind and Inuit people in North America are Christians and they are "full fledged members of the Church, although not of society." They have discovered in their own cultures "special ways" of living their relationship with God and with the world.

Far from destroying the "authentic values and customs" of these native peoples, the Gospel has "the power to purify and uplift" their cultural heritage. Throughout history, the "Church herself has been constantly enriched" by such new traditions.

The encounter with the Gospel does not destroy what is best in native culture but "enriches as it were from within the spiritual qualities and gifts that are distinctive" of these cultures.

"Il cristianesimo non solo è importante per le populazioni native: Cristo, nel corpo, è un Indiano." E Papa Giovanni Paolo II ci ricorda che il Vangelo "ci invita a vivere come fratelli e sorelle di Cristo."

Molte popolazioni amerinde e inuite nell'America del nord sono cristiane e sono "membri a pieno diritto della Chiesa, anche se non della società." Esse hanno scoperto nelle proprie culture "dei modi particolari" di vivere il loro rapporto con Dio e con il mondo.

Lungi del distruggere "gli autentici valori e tradizioni" di questi popoli nativi, il Vangelo ha "il potere di purificare e innalzare" la loro eredità culturale. E nel corso della storia, "la Chiesa stessa è stata costantemente arricchita" da tali nuove tradizioni.

L'incontro con il Vangelo non distrugge ciò che di meglio esiste nella cultura nativa, ma, al contrario, "l'arricchisce come se scaturisse dalla natura stessa delle qualità e dei doni spirituali che sono distintivi" di queste culture.

„Chrześcijaństwo, dla rdzennej ludności „nie tylko posiada znaczenie, lecz Chrystus, w członach swego Ciała, jest Indianinem". I Papież Jan Paweł II przypomina nam, że Ewangelia „wzywa nas do życia jak bracia i siostry".

Wiele jest chrześcijańskich plemion Amerindów i Inuitów w Północnej Ameryce i są oni „pełnoprawnymi członkami Kościoła, lecz, niestety, nie społeczeństwa". Znaleźli w swoich kulturach „szczególne drogi" utrzymania łączności z Bogiem i światem.

Daleko od zniszczenia „autentycznych wartości i obyczajów" tych rdzennych narodów, Ewangelia jest w mocy „oczyścić i podźwignąć" ich kulturowe dziedzictwo. I w przeciągu wieków, Kościół sam był wzbogacany" przez nowe tradycje.

Spotkanie z Ewangelią, nie niszczy tego, co jest najlepsze w kulturze tubylców, lecz „wzbogaca do pewnego stopnia i obdarza wartoscią duchową".

Z kolei, tradycje Amerindów i Inuitów, proprzez znajdywanie nowych dróg wyrażania nowiny zbawienia, „pomagają nam lepiej zrozumieć" rolę Jezusa i uniwersalności zbawienia.

À leur tour, les traditions amérindiennes et inuit en permettant de nouvelles expressions du message du Salut, "nous aident à mieux comprendre" le rôle de Jésus et l'universalité du Salut.

Les valeurs morales et spirituelles des peuples autochtones sont, entre autres, le sens aigu de la présence de Dieu, l'amour de la famille, le respect des personnes âgées, la solidarité avec leur propre peuple, le partage, l'hospitalité, le respect de la nature allié à la gratitude pour le don de la terre, au souci qu'ils portent à notre planète, et l'importance accordée au silence et à la prière. "Le monde a besoin de ces valeurs." Les laisser s'appauvrir, "ce serait appauvrir aussi les gens" qui [les autochtones] vivent avec les autochtones".

"L'Église n'intervient pas directement dans [le] domaine civil", mais elle se préoccupe des problèmes des autochtones dans la société moderne. Le Christ rend possible la réconciliation entre les peuples, de sorte que même si "les relations entre autochtones et blancs sont encore souvent tendues et empreintes de préjugés", "nous pourrons nous accepter les uns les autres dans nos différences, malgré nos limites et notre péché".

Les autochtones perçoivent les défis et savent en tirer profit. L'histoire prouve qu'ils ont souvent été victimes d'injustices de la part de ceux qui considéraient toute leur culture comme inférieure. "On commence à prendre conscience de l'immense richesse de [cette] culture."

L'heure est venue de panser les blessures, de cicatriser les déchirures. "Le moment est venu de pardonner, de se réconcilier et de s'engager à nouer de nouvelles relations."

In turn, the Amerind and Inuit traditions, by developing new ways of expressing the message of salvation "help us to better understand" the role of Jesus and the universality of salvation.

Native moral and spiritual values include an acute sense of the presence of God, love of family, respect for the aged, solidarity with one's own people, sharing, hospitality, respect for nature along with a sense of gratitude for the land and responsible stewardship of the earth, and the love of silence and prayer. "The world needs to see these values." To let them "become impoverished would be to impoverish the people around you."

The Church does not "intervene directly in civil matters" but is concerned over the problems of natives in modern society. Christ makes possible "reconciliation between peoples" so that although relations "between Native people and white people are often strained and tainted with prejudice", we should "be able to accept one another with our differences and despite our limitations and our sins."

But they "perceive the challenges" and "know how to make the most of it." History shows that native people have often been "victims of injustice by … those who … saw all your culture as inferior." We are learning to appreciate that "there is great richness in your culture."

The hour has come to bind up wounds, to heal all divisions. "It is a time for forgiveness, for reconciliation and for a commitment to building new relationships."

Da parte loro le tradizioni amerinde e inuite, rivelando dei nuovi modi di esprimere il messaggio di salvezza, "ci aiutano a comprendere meglio" il ruolo di Gesù e l'universalità della salvezza.

I valori nativi, morali e spirituali, racchiudono in sè un senso profondo della presenza di Dio, l'amore per le famiglie, il rispetto per gli anziani, la solidarietà con il proprio popolo, il senso di comunione con gli altri, l'ospitalità, il rispetto per la natura unito a un senso di gratitudine per la propria terra e di responsabilità verso il mondo, l'amore per il silenzio e la preghiera. "Il mondo ha bisogno di questi valori." "Lasciarli impoverire significherebbe rendere più povera anche la gente intorno a Voi."

La Chiesa non "interviene direttamente in questioni civili," ma essa prende a cuore i problemi dei nativi nella società moderna. Cristo rende possibile "la riconciliazione fra i popoli," cosi che, sebbene le relazioni fra nativi e bianchi siano spesso danneggiate e macchiate dai pregiudizi," noi dobbiamo "essere in grado di accettarci l'un l'altro con tutte le nostre differenze, e malgrado i nostri limiti e peccati."

Ma le popolazioni native "si rendono conto della sfida" e "sanno come trarne il maggior vantaggio possibile." La storie mostra che esse sono spesso state vittime di ingiustizia da parte di … coloro che … consideravano inferiore tutta la vostra cultura." Noi stiamo imparando a riconoscere che "c'è una grande ricchezza nella vostra cultura."

È giunta l'ora di guarire le ferite e di sanare tutte le divisioni. È tempo di perdono, di riconciliazione, e di impegno per l'edificazione di nuovi rapporti."

Moralność tubylców oraz ich wartości duchowe, charakteryzują się zdolnością wyczuwania obecności Boga, miłością do rodziny, szacunkiem do starszych, solidarnością ze współplemieńcami, gościnnością, szacunkiem do przyprody razem z poczuciem wdzięczności za ziemię, rozumnym zarządzaniem ziemią oraz zamiłowaniem do ciszy i modlitwy. „Świat musi poznać te wartości".

Kościół nie „interweniuje bezpośrednio w sprawy państwowe", lecz jest zainteresowany problemami tubylców we współczesnym społeczeństwie. Chrystus umożliwia „pojednanie między ludźmi" dlatego też, pomimo to, że stosunki „między rdzenną ludnością i białymi często są napięte i splamione uprzedzeniem", powinniśmy „być gotowi do zaakceptowania jeden drugiego z naszymi różnicami, niedoskonałością i grzechami".

Historia dowodzi, że rdzenna ludność, często padała ofiarą niesprawiedliwości … tych, którzy … uważali Waszą kulturę sa niższą. Uczymy się doceniać „bogactwo Waszej kultury".

Nadszedł czas opatrzyć rany, usunąć wszystkie niezgody. To jest czas na przebaczenie, pojednanie oraz zobowiazanie do nawiązania nowych stosunków".

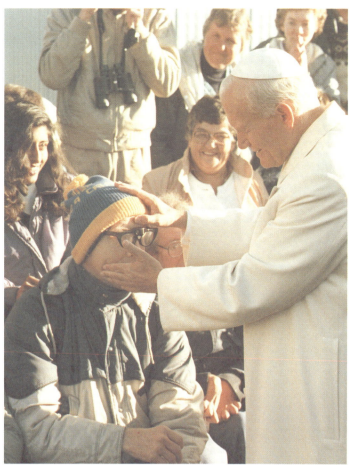

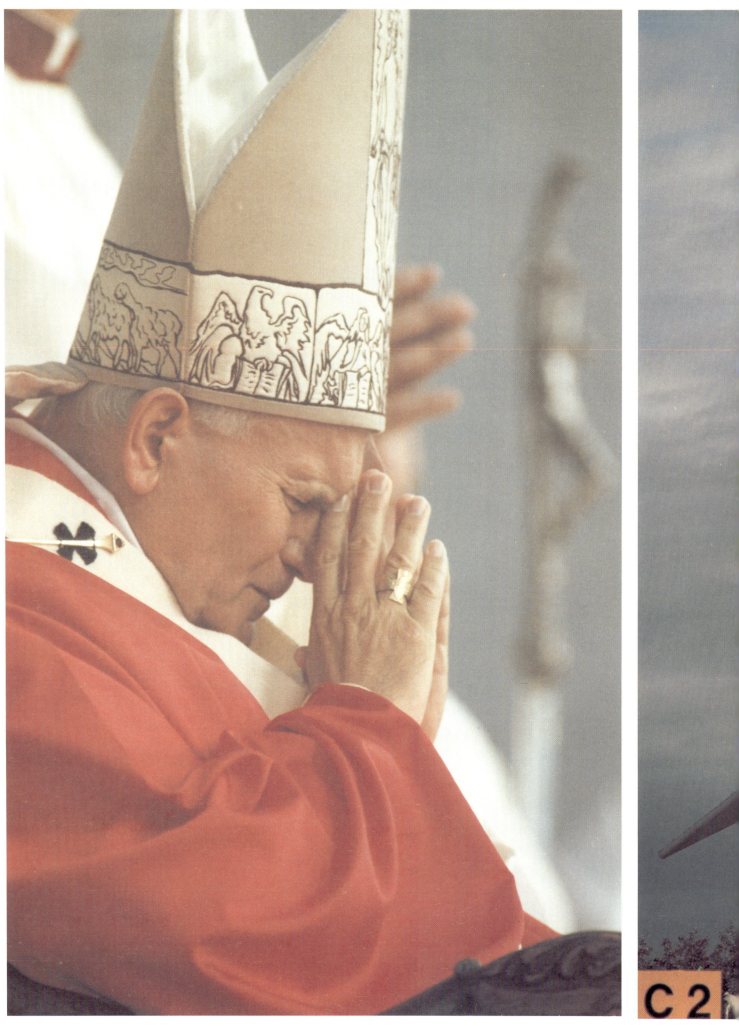

C 2

Le mystère de Dieu en Jésus-Christ

Mystery of God in Jesus Christ

Mistero di Dio in Gesù Cristo

Tajemnica Boża w Jezusie Chrystusie

"Je suis venu à vous pour proclamer Jésus-Christ." Le Pape Jean-Paul II nous parle du "mystère de son Sacré-Coeur".

"Lorsque nous parlons du 'Coeur de Jésus-Christ', nous nous adressons par notre foi au mystère christologique tout entier : le mystère de Dieu-Homme."

"Le Fils est un en substance avec le Père. Il est Dieu de Dieu." C'est le mystère au centre de la foi chrétienne.

"Le coeur en effet est un organe humain qui appartient au corps, qui fait partie de toute la structure, de la composition spirituelle et physique de l'homme."

Il a une signification comme organe, mais aussi comme "centre symbolique du moi intérieur", spirituel par essence. Pendant la vie terrestre de Jésus, son Coeur était le "centre dans lequel se manifestait, d'une façon humaine, l'amour de Dieu".

Le don le plus important, le plus profond de ce coeur est que les hommes et les femmes reçoivent "le pouvoir de devenir des enfants de Dieu".

Toute la création, toute l'humanité marche vers Dieu à travers le Christ. "Le Coeur de Jésus-Christ est une invitation de Dieu, sans cesse renouvelée, qui s'adresse à l'humanité et à chaque coeur humain."

"I have come to you to proclaim Jesus Christ." Pope John Paul II speaks to us of the "mystery of his Sacred Heart."

When we speak of the "heart" of Jesus "we address ourselves in faith to the whole Christological mystery: the mystery of the God–Man."

The Son is "one in substance" with the Father, he is "God from God." This is the mystery at the heart of the Christian faith.

But the "heart is a human organ, belonging to the body, belonging to the whole structure, to the spiritual and physical make-up of man."

It has meaning as an organ, but also as "the symbolic centre of the inner self", which is, by nature, spiritual. During Christ's earthly life his heart was the "centre, in which was manifested, in a human way," the love of God.

The most important and profound gift of this heart is that humanity is given "the power to become the children of God."

All creation, and all humanity, moves toward God through Christ. The Heart of Jesus is "a great and unceasing call from God, addressed to humanity, to each human heart."

"Sono venuto a voi per proclamare Gesù Cristo." Papa Giovanni Paolo II ci parla del "mistero del Sacro Cuore di Gesù."

Quando parliamo del "cuore" di Gesù "ci indirizziamo con fede all'intero mistero cristologico; il mistero del Dio fatto Uomo."

Il Figlio è "delle stesse sostanze" del Padre, Egli è "Dio da Dio." Questo è il mistero che è il cuore della fede cristiana.

Ma "il cuore è un organo umano, che fa parte del corpo, all'intera struttura, alla costituzione spirituale e fisica dell'uomo."

esso ha una funzione in quanto organo, ma anche in quanto "centro simbolico dell'io interiore," che è, per sua propria natura, spirituale. Nella vita terrena di Cristo, il Suo cuore era "il centro in cui si manifestava umanamente," l'amore di Dio.

Il dono più importante e completo del Suo cuore consiste nell'aver concesso agli uomini "di potere diventare figli di Dio."

Tutta la creazione e tutta l'umanità si muovono verso Dio attraverso Cristo. Il cuore di Gesù è un "grande e incessante appello di Dio rivolto all'umanità ed a ogni cuore umano."

„Przyjechałem do Was, aby ogłosić Jezusa Chrystusa". Papież Jan Paweł II mówi o „tajemnicy Jego Świętego Serca".

Kiedy mówimy o „sercu Jezusa, „zwracamy się w wierze" do całej tajemnicy chrystusowej: tajemnicy Boga–Człowieka".

Syn i Ojciec w „jednej osobie", On jest „Bogiem z Boga". To jest tajemnica serca wiary chrześcijańskiej.

Lecz „serce to organ ludzki, należący do ciała, należący do całego układu, do duchowej i fizycznej natury człowieka.

Jest ono organem, lecz również jest „symbolem życia wewnętrznego", które jest, z natury, duchowe. Podczas życia Chrystusa na ziemi, Jego serce było „centrum, w którym ujawniła się, w sposób ludzki, miłość Boga.

Najważniejszym i całkowitym darem Tego serca, jest to, że ludzkości jest dana „moc stać się dziećmi Boga".

Cały świat i cała ludzkość podąża do Boga poprzez Chrystusa. Serce Chrystusa, jest głośnym i nieustającym wołaniem od Boga, skierowanym do ludzkości, do każdego ludzkiego serca".

La paix

Peace

Pace

Pokój

"Nous prions pour la paix, et le chemin de la paix passe par la justice." Le Pape Jean-Paul II, au terme de son pèlerinage, nous rappelle les liens qui existent entre la justice et la paix, et les "droits inviolables de l'homme et des nations".

Mais "le point de départ des voies qui conduisent à la justice et à la paix se trouve dans la Rédemption du monde" par le Christ. "Et c'est seulement à la lumière de la Croix et de la Résurrection que ce qui est humain, ce qui est héroïque en l'homme retrouve sa force et sa puissance." Nous pouvons devenir des "disciples du Christ et de véritables frères et soeurs entre nous" en prenant part à la marche de la civilisation sur la voie de la justice et de la paix, en devenant des défenseurs de la paix.

Nous devons être "les défenseurs d'une conception nouvelle de l'humanité", et considérer les problèmes de société "en fonction des

"We pray for peace, and the way to peace is through justice." At the end of his pilgrimage, Pope John Paul reminds us of the links between justice and peace and the "inviolable rights of individuals and of nations."

But the "way to justice and peace begins with the redemption of the world" through Christ. It is "in the light of the cross and the resurrection that what is human and heroic in human beings will recover its strength and its power." We can become "disciples of Christ and true brothers and sisters among ourselves" by taking part in the "thrust of civilization" towards justice and peace, by becoming "peacemakers".

We need to be "bearers of a new vision of humanity" seeing society's problems "in terms of living people, of human beings created in the image and likeness of God."

"Noi preghiamo per la pace, e il cammino verso le pace è attraverso la giustizia." Papa Giovanni Paolo II ci ricorda, alla fine del suo pellegrinaggio, del vincolo fra giustizia e pace, e dei "diritti inviolabili degli individui e delle nazioni."

Ma "il cammino verso la giustizia e le pace comincia con la redenzione del mondo" attraverso Cristo. È alla luce della croce e della Resurrezione che ciò che è umano ed eroico negli uomini recupererà forza e potenza." Noi possiamo diventare "discepoli di Cristo e vivere insieme da veri fratelli e sorelle" prendendo parte alla "spinta della civiltà" verso la giustizia e la pace diventando "portatori di pace."

Dobbiamo essere "portatori di una nuova visione di umanità," guardando ai problemi sociali "in termini di persone vive, di esseri umani creati ad immagine e somiglianza di Dio."

La violenza, di qualsiasi tipo sia, è "contraddizione completa" di una vita veramente umana, che dovrebbe essere vissuta "nella saggezza, cultura e moralità." La violenza moderna non solo

„Modlimy się o pokój, a drogą do pokoju, jest sprawiedliwość". Papież Jan Paweł II przypomina nam, na końcu swojej pielgrzymki, o nici łączącej sprawiedliwość i pokój oraz o „nienaruszalnych prawach jednostek i narodów.

Lecz „droga do sprawiedliwości i pokoju, zaczyna się od zbawienia świata poprzez Chrystusa. To jest „w świetle krzyża i zmartwychwstania, że to, co jest ludzkie i bohaterskie w człowieku, odzyska swoją moc i swoją władzę. Możemy zostać „uczniami Chrystusa i prawdziwymi braćmi i siostrami", biorąc udział w „pchnięciu cywilizacji" w kierunku sprawiedliwości i pokoju, stając się „bojownikami o wolność".

Musimy być „nosicielami nowych wizji ludzkości", zauważając problemy społeczeństwa, „mając na uwadze ludzi, człowieka stworzonego na wizerunek i podobieństwo Boga".

Przemoc różnego rodzaju „jest w całkowitej sprzeczności" z prawdziwym ludzkim życiem,

personnes vivantes, des êtres humains créés à l'image et à la ressemblance de Dieu".

Toute violence, quelle qu'elle soit, "contredit complètement 'la véritable vie humaine, qui devrait être vie' de sagesse, de culture, de moralité". La violence moderne "menace de mort tout ce qui est humain". "Ainsi donc, on ne peut permettre que la conscience morale de l'humanité cède à la violence." "Il faut défendre de la mort les hommes", que ce soit par le nucléaire ou par la faim; "il faut défendre de la mort tout ce qui est humain".

Malgré le renouveau de la conscience morale après la Seconde Guerre mondiale, des tensions, des affrontements et des guerres localisées subsistent. "Les sources des conflits se trouvent partout où l'injustice meurtrit, où la dignité de trop d'hommes est bafouée."

Dans le monde entier, il existe de "terribles disparités" entre les riches et les pauvres. Dans le monde entier, on dénie aux hommes leurs convictions personnelles et religieuses, leurs "libertés civiles". De plus, la spirale de la course aux armements constitue non seulement une menace réelle, mais "son coût économique prive tant de pays des moyens effectifs de leur développement".

"Au milieu de la famille humaine menacée, le Christ se tient sans cesse comme Prince-de-la-Paix, comme Défenseur de ce qui est humain."

Nous devons chercher sans répit le chemin de la paix, mais la paix entre les peuples du monde "sera toujours précaire si nous ne sommes pas en paix avec Dieu, si nous ne nous conformons pas, au plus intime de notre être, au plan de Dieu sur toute l'histoire du monde".

Violence of any kind "is in complete contradiction" to a true human life, which should be lived "by wisdom, by culture, and by morality." Not only does modern violence "threaten to kill human beings" it threatens "to destroy all that is human." And we "cannot permit the moral conscience of humanity to give in" to this violence. We must "protect people from death" whether from nuclear death or starvation, we must "protect from death all that is human."

Despite a renewal of moral consciousness since World War Two, tensions and conflicts and local wars have continued. "The sources of the conflicts are found wherever injustice kills, or wherever the dignity of people is scoffed at."

All over the world "frightful disparities" exist between rich and poor. All over the world men are denied their personal and religious beliefs and their "civil liberties." Besides this, the spiral of the arms race is not only a real threat but "its economic cost deprives so many countries of the effective means for their development."

"In the midst of this threatened human family, Christ continues to stand as the Prince of Peace, as the Defender of all that is human."

We must seek the way to peace "untiringly" but peace among all the peoples of the world will be "precarious if we are not at peace with God, if we do not conform ourselves in our inmost being to the plan of God for the history of the world".

"minaccia di uccidere esseri umani," essa minaccia anche "di distruggere tutto ciò che è umano. E noi "non possiamo permettere che la coscienza morale dell'umanità si arrende a questa violenza." Dobbiamo "proteggere i popoli dalla morte," sia che si tratti della morte nucleare o della morte per fame, dobbiamo "proteggere dalla morte tutto ciò che è umano."

Nonostante un rinnovamento della coscienze morale avvenuto a partire dalla seconda guerra mondiale, sono continuati tensioni, conflitti, e guerre locali. "Le radici dei conflitti si trovano ovunque l'ingiustizia uccida, o ovunque si calpesti la dignità dei popoli."

E in tutto il mondo esistono "spaventose disparità" fra ricchi e poveri. In tutto il mondo si negano agli uomini le loro fedi personali e religiose e le loro "libertà civili." Inoltre, il vortice della corsa agli armamenti non solo è una reale minaccia, ma "i suoi costi economici sottraggono anche a molti paesi i mezzi effettivi per il loro sviluppo."

"Al centro di questa umana famiglia minacciata, Cristo continua a ergersi a Principe delle Pace, a Difensore di tutto ciò che è umano."

Dobbiamo cercare la vie per la pace "instancabilmente," ma la pace fra tutti i popoli della terra sarà "precaria se non saremo in pace con Dio, se non ci conformeremo al disegno divino della storia del mondo."

któremu powinny przyświecać "mądrość, kultura, moralność". Przemoc nie tylko "zagraża życiu człowieka", lecz również "wszystkiemu, co jest ludzkie". Nie możemy nawet dopuścić do naszej świadomości człowieczej myśli o nie reagowaniu na tą przemoc. Musimy "chronić ludzi od śmierci" niezależnie, czy śmierci od bomby nuklearnej, czy też od głodu, musimy "chronić od śmierci wszystko, co jest ludzkie".

Niezależnie od odnowy moralnej świadomosci po drugiej wojnie światowej, istnieją nadal napięcia, konflikty i wojny lokalne. "Źródła konfliktów znajdujemy wszędzie, gdzie zabija niesprawiedliwość lub tam, gdzie kpi się z godności ludzkiej"

Na całym świecie istnieją "przerażające różnice" między bogatymi i biednymi. Na całym świecie człowiekowi odmawia się jego praw do osobistej i religijnej wiary oraz jego "wolności obywatelskich". Poza tym, spirala wyścigów zbrojnych, jest nie tylko prawdziwym zagrożeniem, lecz również "koszty tych zbrojeń pozbawiają wiele krajów skutecznych środków dla ich rozwoju".

Pośród zagrożonej rodziny człowieczej, Chrystus nadal stoi jako Anioł Pokoju, jako Obrońca tego, co jest ludzkie".

Musimy "niezmordowanie" szukać dróg do osiągnięcia pokoju, lecz pokój pomiędzy narodami na całym świecie będzie "wątpliwy, jeżeli nie będziemy w pokoju z Bogiem, jeżeli nie dostosujemy się w naszym najskrytszym bytowaniu, do planów Boga dla dziejów świata".

160

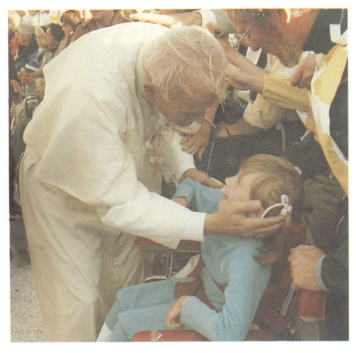

. . . Restez les chercheurs de la vérité.
Déployez avec courage
les richesses qui sont en vous . . .

. . . Remain seekers after truth.
Use with courage the
rich gifts that are within you . . .

. . . Siate ricercatori della verità.
Usatè con coraggio
i ricchi doni che sono in voi . . .

. . . Pozostańcie poszukiwaczami prawdy.
Z odwagą wykorzystujcie bogate dary,
które w Was się znajdują . . .

... Soyez les défenseurs
d'une conception nouvelle
de l'humanité ...

... Be bearers of a new vision
of humanity ...

... Siate portatori
di una nuova visione
di umanità ...

... Bądźcie nosicielami
nowych wizji ludzkości ...

175

... La qualité d'une société ou d'une civilisation
se mesure au respect qu'elle manifeste
envers les plus faibles de ses membres. ...

... The quality of a society or civilization is
measured by the respect it has for its
weakest members ...

... Le qualità di una società o civiltà sono
misurate dal rispetto mostrato per i
deboli ...

... Miarą wartości społeczeńtwa, czy też
cywilizacji, jest respekt, jakim darzeni są
ich najsłabsi członkowie ...

... Votre foi [...] devra
apprendre à se dire
et à se vivre...

... You must learn to
articulate your faith
and to live it...

... Dovete imparare ad
articolare ed a
vivere la vostra
fede...

... Musicie nauczyć się
jasno wyrażać swoją
wiarę i żyć według
jej przykazań...

189

193

... Je souhaite que votre souci
de la paix mondiale fasse
de vous des ouvriers de paix ...

... I want your concern for world peace
to make of you workers for peace ...

... Voglio che la vostra preoccupazione
per la pace nel mondo vi renda
portatori di pace ...

... Pragnę, aby Wasza troska o pokój
na świecie, zrodziła z Was
bojowników o pokój ...

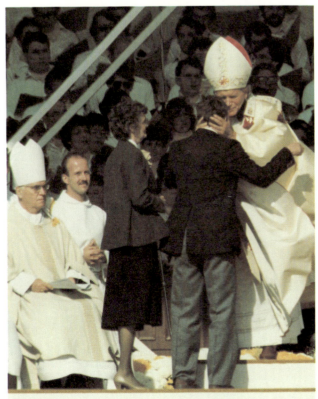

... Vous avez devant vous
beaucoup de tâches exaltantes ...

... You have before you
many challenging tasks ...

... Avete difronte a voi
molte dure prove ...

... Masz przed sobą wiele
trudnych zadań ...

... Nous avons célébré ensemble,
nous avons prié le Seigneur ...

... We have celebrated together,
we have prayed to the Lord ...

... Abbiamo celebrato insieme,
abbiamo pregato Dio ...

... Świętowaliśmy razem,
modliliśmy się do Pana ...

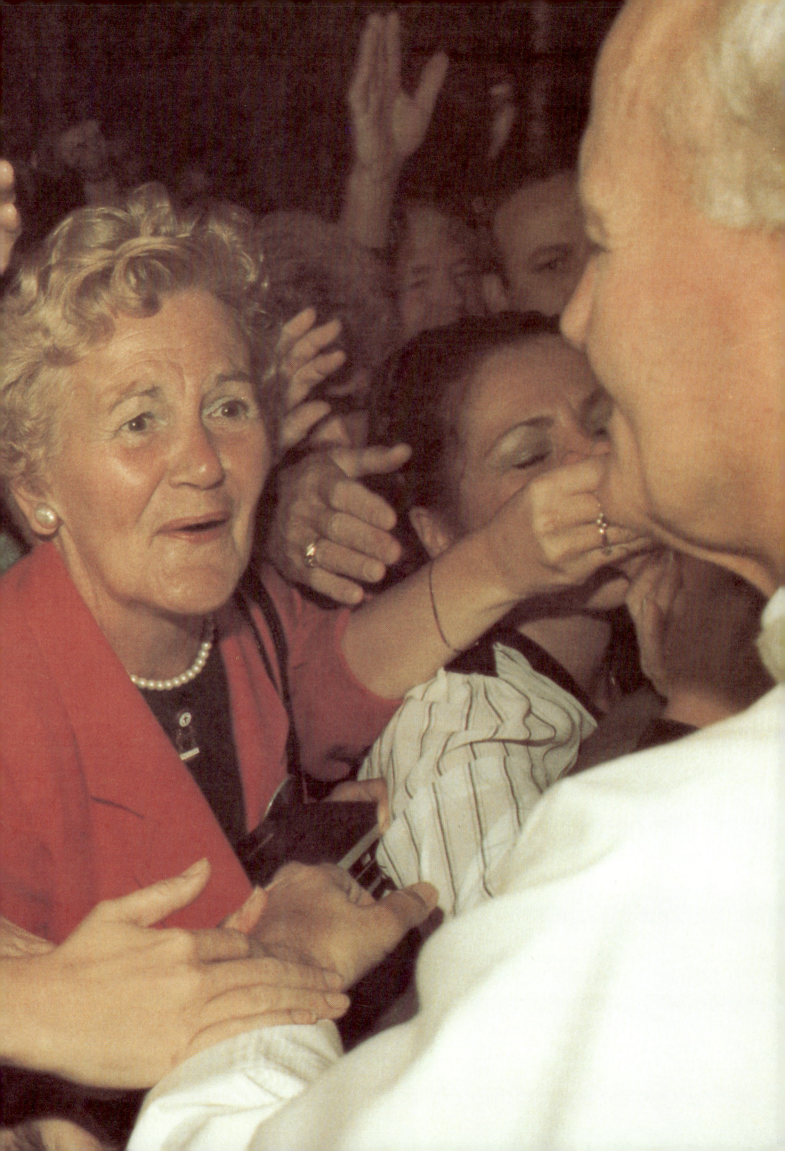

Épilogue

Afterword

Epilogo

Posłowie

À la fin de son long périple, le Pape s'adressait à un groupe hétérogène : représentants officiels pour la plupart, mais aussi personnes qui l'avaient aidé pendant son voyage, la conférence des évêques du Canada, et des personnes habitant dans le voisinage (familles des militaires vivant sur la base où attendait l'avion). Il dit :

"Je me suis invité pour un second voyage."

Les applaudissements et les cris de joie furent sincères. En ce moment précis, tout fut oublié : le rythme incroyable des déplacements, les problèmes de sécurité, les préparatifs innombrables qui ont exigé tant de temps et d'énergie.

Mais ces cris de joie et d'approbation étaient aussi mitigés, car tous savaient bien qu'il est peu probable qu'un tel voyage se reproduise jamais. Il n'en est que plus important sans doute et, tel l'oasis dans le désert, n'en est que plus rare.

Le Pape Jean-Paul II s'est beaucoup dépensé pour nous pendant ces douze jours. Cela évoque des phrases qu'il a prononcées au début de sa visite :

"Je ne suis pas venu vous dévoiler un secret. Je suis venu en témoin, comme Jean le Baptiste était là pour rendre témoignage à la lumière. Je suis venu vous inviter à ouvrir les yeux sur la lumière de la vie, sur le Christ Jésus."

"Si nous écoutons sa parole, si nous le suivons, si nous découvrons la grandeur de l'amour dont il aime tous les hommes et toutes les femmes de tous les âges, alors nous saurons que la vie vaut la peine d'être vécue, et mieux encore d'être donnée."

There was a moment at the end of this long journey. He was speaking to a mixed group – mostly public officials, but also the people who had helped him on his trip, the assembled bishops of Canada, and a group of local residents – the families of the servicemen who live on the base where the plane was waiting.

"I have invited myself for a second trip," he said.

The applause and cheers were genuine. At that moment the incredible pace of the trip, the security problems, the massive preparations that took so much time and energy, all were forgotten.

But the cheer and the approval was tinged with the knowledge that such a trip was unlikely to happen, ever again. Perhaps that makes it more important – like an oasis in a desert, we see clearly because it is so rare.

Pope John Paul II gave much of himself to us during these twelve days, and it brings to mind his words from early in the visit:

"I have not come to reveal a secret to you. I have come as a witness, as John the Baptist came, to witness to the light. I have come to invite you to open your eyes to the light of life, to Christ Jesus.

"If we listen to his word, if we follow him, if we discover the greatness of his love for all men and all women of every age, then we will know that life is worth living, and better still, that it is worth giving."

È stato un attimo alla fine di questa lunga visita. Parlava a un gruppo vario di persone – in maggioranza pubblici funzionari, ma anche alla gente che lo aveva aiutato nel corso del viaggio, ai vescovi canadesi riuniti, e a un gruppo di residenti locali – le famiglie dei membri delle forze armate che vivevono nella base dove l'attendeva l'aereo.

"Mi sono autoinvitato a tornare per una seconda visita," ha detto.

Gli applausi e le acclamazioni erano sinceri. In quell'attimo, l'incredibile ritmo del viaggio, i problemi di sicurezza, gli imponenti preparativi che avevano richiesto tanto tempo e tanta fatica, tutto era dimenticato.

Ma le acclamazioni e i consensi erano misti alla consapevolezza che una tale visita, probabilmente, non si sarebbe ripetuta mai più. Forse, in un certo modo, ciò la rende più importante – come un'oasi nel deserto, la vediamo chiaramente perchè è così rara.

Papa Giovanni Paolo II ci ha dato molto di se stesso durante questi dodici giorni, e vengono in mente le parole pronunciate all'inizio della visita: "Non sono venuto per rivelarvi un segreto. Sono venuto per testimoniare, come Giovanni Battista, della luce. Sono venuto per invitarvi ad aprire gli occhi alla luce della vita, a Cristo Gesù.

Se ascolteremo la Sua parola, se Lo seguiremo, se scopriremo la grandezza del Suo amore per tutti gli uomini e le donne di ogni età, allora sapremo che la vita è degna di essere vissuta o, ancora di più, degna di essere donata."

Był moment na końcu tej długiej podróży. Przemawiał do różnorodnych grup – w większości do przedstawicieli państwowych, lecz również do tych, którzy pomagali mu w czasie jego wizyty, do zgromadzonych biskupów kanadyjskich, do grupy okolicznych mieszkańcow – rodzin pracowników bazy, na której stał oczekujący go samolot.

„Zaprosiłem się z wizytą po raz drugi", – powiedział.

Aplauz i radosne okrzyki były szczere. W tym momencie, stało się coś niewiarygodnego – problemy z bezpieczeństwem, wielkie przygotowania, które pochłonęły tyle czasu i energii – wszystko poszło w zapomnienie.

Lecz radość i uznanie były przyćmione świadomością, że tego rodzaju wizyta może nie zdażyć się nigdy już więcej. Być może, właśnie ta świadomość, czyni tą wizytę bardziej ważną – jak oazę na pustyni, widzimy wyraźnie, gdyż jest tak rzadka.

Papież Jan Paweł II dał nam z siebie wszystko w ciągu tych dwunastu dni i to przypomina jego słowa z początku podróży:

„Nie przyjechałem, aby odkryć sekret przed Wami. Przyjechałem jako świadek, tak jak Jan Baptysta, dać dowód Światłu. Przyjechałem, żeby zachęcić Was do otwarcia oczu na Światło życia, na Jezusa Chrystusa".

„Jeżeli słuchamy Jego słów, jeżeli podążamy za Nim, jeżeli odkrywamy ogrom Jego miłości do wszystkich meżczyzn i kobiet w róznym wieku, wtedy będziemy wiedzieć, że życie warte jest życia, to znaczy, że warte jest poświęcenia."

Remerciements particuliers

Special Acknowledgements

Ringraziamenti speciali

Specjalne Podziękowanie

Rev. Francis Abbass
Michael J. E. Amy
John D. Appleby
Melvin L. Boys
Robert P. Birt
Keith Campbell
Mrs. Dorothy de la Plante
Gino della Rocca
Jacques Emond
Muriel Frazier
Charles D. Frazier
Richard Gareau Sr.
Frank Gilhooley
David Goodman
Doreen Gough
Mike Gough
Rev. Regis Halloran
David G. Heeley
John G. Hewitt
Adrian Hines
Diane Houston
Charles Kitts
Père Gérard Laprise, OMI
John Lawlor
Mike Lawlor
Kimberley Mearns
Richard McCorkell
Jack G. McIntyre
William R. McMurtry Q.C.
Monsignor Dennis J. Murphy
Allan Pratt
Rev. Bernard A. Prince
Tony Scapillati
Rodney L. K. Smith Q.C.
Jean A. Van Neste
Linda A. Waddington